AMṚTĀṢṬAKAM

A Vedāntic Inquiry Into Supreme Devotion

A Commentary on Eight Verses
From the Bhagavad-Gītā
With Examples From the Life & Teachings
of Sri Mata Amritanandamayi Devi

By Swami Ramakrishnananda Puri

Mata Amritanandamayi Center
San Ramon, California, USA

Amṛtāṣṭakam: A Vedāntic Inquiry Into Supreme Devotion

A Commentary on Eight Verses From the Bhagavad-Gītā
With Examples From the Life & Teachings of Sri Mata Amritanandamayi Devi
By Swami Ramakrishnananda Puri

Published By:
Mata Amritanandamayi Center
P.O. Box 613, San Ramon, CA 94583-0613 USA
www.amma.org
www.theammashop.org

First printing: May 2016, 2,000 copies

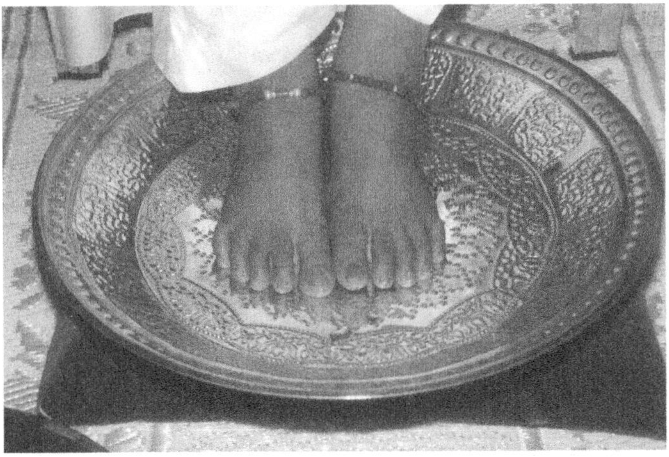

Offered at the Lotus Feet
of my Sadguru, Śrī Mātā Amṛtānandamayī Devī

Contents

Śrī Mātā Amṛtānandamayī Devī	6
Introduction	7
Śrī Ādi Śaṅkarācārya	19
Amṛtāṣṭakam	20
One Who Hates No Being	22
A Friend	31
A Compassionate Person	38
One Without a Sense of "Mine"	47
One Without a Separate Sense of "I"	52
One Who Is the Same in Hardship & Comfort	58
One Endowed With Forgiveness	65
One Who Is Ever Content	74
One Whose Mind Is Concentrated	79
One Who Is Self-controlled	82
One Who Is of Firm Conviction	88
One Whose Mind & Intellect Are Fixed in Me	94
One From Whom the World Cowers Not & Who Cowers Not From the World	99
One Who Is Devoid of Elation, Non-forbearance, Fear & Anxiety	109
One Who Is Devoid of Desires	112
One Who Is Pure	119
One Who Is Efficient	123
One Who Is Impartial	126
One Who Is Free From Emotional Pain	130
One Who Has Renounced All Undertakings	133

One Who Neither Rejoices,
Hates, Grieves Nor Desires 136

One Who Has Renounced the
Auspicious & The Inauspicious 137

One Who Views Friend & Foe,
Honor & Dishonor, Heat & Cold,
and the Comfortable &
Uncomfortable With Equanimity 153

One Who Is Free From Attachment 157

One Who Remains the Same
in the Face of Censure & Praise 158

One Who Is Silent 159

One Who Is Content With Anything 161

One Who Is Homeless 163

One Who Is Firm in Knowledge 167

Concluding Verse 169

Pronunciation Guide 174

Śrī Mātā Amṛtānandamayī Devī

Through her extraordinary acts of love and self-sacrifice, Śrī Mātā Amṛtānandamayī Devī, or "Amma" [Mother], as she is more commonly known, has endeared herself to millions around the world. Tenderly caressing everyone who comes to her, holding them close to her heart in a loving embrace, Amma shares her boundless love with all—regardless of their beliefs, their social status or why they have come to her. In this simple yet powerful way, Amma is transforming the lives of countless people, helping their hearts to blossom, one embrace at a time. In the past 40 years, Amma has physically hugged more than 36 million people from all parts of the world.

Her tireless spirit of dedication to uplifting others has inspired a vast network of charitable activities, through which people are discovering the deep sense of peace and inner fulfillment that comes from selflessly serving others. Amma teaches that the divine exists in everything, sentient and insentient. Realizing this truth is the essence of spirituality—the means to end all suffering. Amma's teachings are universal. Whenever she is asked about her religion, she replies that her religion is love. She does not ask anyone to believe in God or to change their faith, but only to inquire into their own real nature and to believe in themselves.

Introduction

In India, enlightened masters like Amma are referred to by many different terms. There is *siddha*—a perfected one; *jīvanmukta*—one liberated while alive; *mahātmā*—a great soul... However, perhaps the most revealing name is *ātma-jñānī*—a knower of the self. This name is revealing because it shows us the secret behind what makes someone like Amma so special—the secret that makes her so loving, so compassionate, so peaceful, so selfless and blissful. That secret is that Amma knows who she truly is.

THE IMPORTANCE OF KNOWLEDGE

When we study the Indian scriptures, we see that they stress the importance of knowledge—its power to completely transform our lives, its power to completely change the way we perceive the world, its power to change the way we act. This is because our understanding of people, places, things, situations, etc, forms the foundation upon which our entire life is constructed. Just as every figurine produced from a faulty mold will likewise be faulty, so too it is with a life founded on faulty understanding. In the scriptures we find many examples of this phenomenon: the misunderstanding of the rope to be a snake, the misunderstanding of the post to be a ghost, the misunderstanding of the mother of pearl to be silver, etc. What these examples demonstrate is that when we misunderstand something's nature, we live our lives with a misinformed attitude toward that thing, which in turn leads to misinformed action.

In my youth I saw what is now considered a classic Clint Eastwood Western, *The Good, the Bad & The Ugly* (1966), which provides us with a modern example of this principle. During the American Civil War, the Union soldiers wore blue and the Confederate soldiers wore gray. In the film, two fugitives of no particular military allegiance are trying to escape arrest by disguising themselves in stolen Confederate uniforms. Driving their wagon through the dusty terrain, they see an army approaching in the distance. They stop their wagon in panic.

Are they wearing gray or blue? Should they keep on their gray disguises or remove them? As the army comes closer, they see the soldiers are wearing gray. The fugitives relax and begin shouting out to their "brothers in arms," "*Hoorah! Hoorah* for the Confederacy! *Hoorah!* Down with General Grant! *Hoorah* for General Lee!" Alas, when the troops stop and start dusting off their uniforms, they reveal their true colors—they are really just Bluecoats covered in dust from the trail. By then, it is too late for the conmen to even try to escape.

When the fugitives were unclear about the nature of the army, their attitude was one of uncertainty, resulting in the action of stopping and waiting. When they misunderstood the army to be friendly, their attitude became one of elation, resulting in the action of waving and cheering. And when they finally understood the army to be the enemy, their attitude became one of fear, which, had there been time, would have caused them to try to flee.

The principle revealed here is the reason the Upaniṣads, Bhagavad-Gītā and other scriptures stress the importance of *ātma-jñānam*—self-knowledge. They tell us that we humans are born with a misunderstanding of our own nature, and it is this misunderstanding that is the foundation of all of our problematic attitudes and actions. In essence, we believe ourselves to be the finite body-mind-sense complex—a limited individual that is born, lives a certain number of years of emotional dependency on unstable objects, and then perishes. The scriptures boldly proclaim that nothing could be further from the truth—that, in reality, we are all the infinite, all-pervasive, unindividualized consciousness, which was never born, never dies and is of the nature of perpetual, causeless bliss. India's spiritual tradition is confident that if we correct this misunderstanding—that is, if we can become *ātma-jñānīs* like Amma—we can radically transform our lives for the better, replacing our sorrow, tension and agitation with bliss, peace and contentment. As the Upaniṣad boldly proclaims: *tarati śokam ātma-vit*—"The one who knows himself crosses over sorrow."[1]

[1] Chāndogya Upaniṣad, 7.1.3

STUDYING THE CHARACTERISTICS OF THE ĀTMA-JÑĀNĪ

In the Bhagavad-Gītā, there are several sections wherein Śrī Kṛṣṇa provides us with descriptions of the virtues, attitudes and general behavioral characteristics found in the *ātma-jñānī*. These include the description of the *sthitaprajña* in the second chapter, the description of the *parābhakta* in the 12th chapter, the indications of *jñānam* in the 13th chapter and of the *guṇātīta* in the 14th chapter.[1] Although Kṛṣṇa uses different Sanskrit terminologies, in each section he is describing one and the same thing: the *ātma-jñānī*—someone who thoroughly understands his divine nature. Thus, the qualities enumerated in these sections—such as compassion, patience, mental control, etc—are, in fact, products of self-knowledge. Thus, *ātma-jñānam* is the cause; the virtuous, noble qualities the effect.

For spiritual aspirants like ourselves, who possess at least a basic understanding of the fact that self-knowledge is the only means to lasting peace and happiness and who thus desire to become *ātma-jñānīs*, studying these behaviors and attitudes is very beneficial. First of all, such study helps us gain insight into the very nature of that which we are striving to attain. For example, in the second chapter of the Gītā, Kṛṣṇa says an *ātma-jñānī* will be free of attachment, fear and anger.[2] Through our study we can come to understand exactly why self-knowledge destroys these negativities. What is the understanding that has arisen in the *ātma-jñānī* about himself that has negated them? What exactly is the connection between the two? If attaining self-knowledge is the primary goal of our life, these are questions we must investigate. We must come to understand the nature of *ātma-jñānam* to the fullest extent possible.

Another reason it is helpful to study these sections of the Gītā is that, according to the scriptures, all the various virtues that are natural behavior for the *ātma-jñānī* should be taken as spiritual

1 Respectively, 2.55-57 and 2.69-2.71, 12.13-19, 13.8-12 and 14.19-25. These translate as "the person of steady wisdom," "supreme devotee," "knowledge," and "one who has transcended the guṇas."

2 Gītā, 2.69: vīta-rāga-bhaya-krodhaḥ

disciplines by the spiritual aspirant. As Śrī Ādi Śaṅkarācārya writes in his commentary on the Gītā:

> For in all the spiritual scriptures, whatever are the characteristics of the enlightened person are themselves presented as the spiritual practices for the spiritual aspirant. [1]

Furthermore, it is said that unless one has cultivated these qualities, one can never hope to attain *ātma-jñānam*. Initially, this sounds confusing. We come to Amma and tell her that we are fed up with our behavior and want to change; we want to transcend our likes and dislikes and become a more loving, compassionate and peaceful person. Amma tells us the only way to truly do so is to attain self-knowledge. Then we ask Amma how to attain self-knowledge, and she tells us, "First, overcome your likes and dislikes and become more loving and compassionate and peaceful." It sounds like a paradox.

We have to understand this in the proper way. The qualities enumerated in these sections of the Gītā are effects of self-knowledge. This means that when one has understood and assimilated his true nature, these virtues will naturally and spontaneously shine forth to their full capacity. However, *ātma-jñānam* is exactly what it says it is: a type of *jñānam*—knowledge. True, it is an extremely subtle form of knowledge, but it is knowledge nonetheless, and all forms of knowledge—no matter how subtle or how gross, no matter how spiritual or material—occur only in one place: the intellect. Gross knowledge—say, the ability to tie one's shoes or to remember the name of your brother-in-law—doesn't require a very refined mind to assimilate. However, *ātma-jñānam* is said by Kṛṣṇa to be *rāja-vidyā rāja-guhyam*—the king of all knowledge and the most subtle.[2] Thus, if one hopes to fully understand and assimilate self-knowledge, an extremely subtle and refined mind is required. Therefore, until one

---

1 From Śrī Śaṅkara's introductory commentary to Bhagavad-Gītā, 2.55: sarvatra eva hi adhyātma-śāstre kṛtārtha-lakṣaṇāni yāni tāni eva sādhānani upadiśyante yatnasādhyātvāt.

2 Bhagavad-Gītā, 9.2

has attained these qualities to a relative extent, one's mind will remain inadequate for *ātma-jñānam*. As Śrī Śaṅkarācārya writes:

> The undiscriminating ones, who lack self-control, who have not purified themselves through austerity and control over their senses and mind, who have not desisted from bad conduct, who are not tranquil and are proud by nature, they do not perceive [their true nature], even though they strive to do so with the help of the valid means of knowledge such as the scriptures.[1]

So, the difference is one of degree. In order to prepare the mind for self-knowledge, we first must attain these virtues to a certain level. Attaining them to their full degree prior to attaining self-knowledge is impossible. Attaining them to a relative degree, however, creates a mind capable of understanding and assimilating *ātma-jñānam*. Then, once *ātma-jñānam* is fully assimilated, these qualities will manifest to their full capacity, as we see in Amma. This, in fact, is what Amma is telling us when she says, "Compassion is both the beginning and the culmination of spiritual life."

There are a number of reasons why *ātma-jñānam* is considered so subtle that special mental preparation is required for it. First of all, it is the only form of knowledge that is not about an external object; it is about the subject—about "the knower" himself. Moreover, it is not about the gross aspects of the knower—his preferences and intellectual convictions, etc, which are also objects of perception—but about who he is at his very core, his very substratum. Thus, to understand and affirm the information being presented requires a mind capable of a degree of self-awareness and self-observation unrequired in other fields of study. If the mind is overly agitated or sluggish or psychologically conflicted, the information presented—though remaining valid nonetheless—will be taken more as theoretical instead of as a living, appreciable truth.

---

[1] From Śrī Śaṅkara's commentary on Bhagavad-Gītā, 15.11: yatantaḥ api śāstrādi-pramāṇamaiḥ akṛtātmānaḥ asaṁskṛtātmānaḥ tapasā indriya-yajena ca duścaritād anuparatā aśānta-darpātmānaḥ prayatnaṁ kurvantaḥ api na enaṁ paśyanti acetasaḥ avivekinaḥ |

The majority of the qualities presented in the Gītā are appreciated by all cultures, by all religions. Thus, they are universal values. This is not a coincidence. Values such as compassion, patience, friendliness, etc, are universal because they need not really be taught. I know that I want to be treated by others with compassion, with patience, with friendliness, etc. Due to this inherent self-understanding, we naturally cognize that this desire is there in the hearts of all humankind. Thus, we are born with the Golden Rule etched into our hearts: "Do unto others as you would have them do unto you."[1] Violating this natural law negatively impacts our psyche, creating mental discordance, consciously or subconsciously. It fragments the mind, and a fragmented mind is a broken mind. A broken mind can never hope to understand and assimilate the highest spiritual truth, the ultimate reality of our self, of the universe, and of God. Thus, if we desire to attain *ātma-jñānam*, we must put in efforts to cultivate these values.

Another reason values are required in order to assimilate self-knowledge is that, unlike other forms of knowledge, the full benefit of *ātma-jñānam* is attained only when it has been integrated to the extent that it has become our natural way of thinking. To misconceive that we are the finite body-mind-sense complex is a natural misconception, reinforced by lifetimes of experiences that seem to support this conclusion. Thus, assimilating self-knowledge is a long process that requires dedication—a vigilant inner dialogue that consistently reproaches and corrects self-ignorant actions, words and thoughts. Thus, we must willfully remain aware of the spiritual reality as we go about our life in this material world until that spiritual mode of thinking has become permanent and natural. As Amma says, "Even if you were to fall asleep for 10 days, upon waking up you would still remember who you are—your name, your age, where you live, etc. This same level of awareness must be there with regard to our true nature, the self." Maintaining such self-awareness will not be possible

[1] As stated in the Mahābhārata, Anuśāsana Parva, 114.8: na tat parasya saṁdadhyāt pratikūlaṁ yad-ātmanaḥ | eṣa saṁkṣepato dharmaḥ kāmādanya pravartate || "One should never do that to another which one would regard as offensive to one's own self. This, in brief, is the rule of dharma. Other behavior is due to selfish desires."

for a dull, agitated or psychologically fractured mind. Therefore *ātma-jñānam* requires special preparation.

Another reason it is helpful to study these sections of the Gītā is that the presence, or lack thereof, of these qualities can help us evaluate the degree to which we have assimilated *ātma-jñānam*. As mentioned previously, when one has fully assimilated self-knowledge, these qualities will shine forth spontaneously and naturally. This is because, as we will see in the upcoming chapters, each of these qualities corresponds to a given aspect of self-knowledge. They are attitudes and behaviors founded on a firm understanding of the spiritual reality of our true nature. Just as the one who mistakes the rope for a snake will naturally become fearful and run, so too one who understands the rope to be a rope will naturally remain calm and continue about his business. Similarly, one who has understood, for example, "I am not the body," will not become emotionally disturbed and react if someone makes a disparaging remark about his appearance or if he learns his body is ill. The more we understand and assimilate self-knowledge—that is, the more we intellectually grasp and appreciate the reality of our true nature and uproot habitual thoughts and attitudes based on our previous misunderstanding—the more these virtues will manifest within us. Thus, investigating these qualities provides us with a mirror into which we can gaze, evaluate ourselves, make corrections and progress forward. As sincere spiritual seekers, we need to remain alert and honest about our progress.

As Amma regularly reminds us in this regard, ideally we should maintain a diary in which we monitor our behavior. Amma gives the example of a street vendor who provides for his family by buying and selling small items: "Every night, before going to bed, he will check his profit and loss. If there has been any loss, he will think up ways to avoid further losses the following day. If there has been profit, he will try to think of ways to increase it. Only after these calculations and decisions will he go to sleep. Like this, each day, we should introspect and try to identify our negative reactions. For example, whether we got angry with someone due to our own selfishness, whether we were able to help or love someone selflessly, etc. If we did get angry with someone, we should feel regret and try not to react in the same manner the next day. If we were unable to help someone selflessly, we should try to do so the next day. This kind of introspection, self-reflection and evaluation of our own actions and reactions will definitely help us move forward."

Thus, by studying these sections of the Gītā, we can use our negative reactions to identify the exact defect in our self-knowledge and where we need to put in more effort to uproot our habitual, misinformed attitudes and actions. This should create a heightened awareness, helping us both correct and ultimately eradicate our self-misconceptions.

With regards to this self-evaluation, I would like to mention one more thing. In our evaluation, we should pay attention to three components: the regularity of our lapses, how long our lapses last when they do occur, and their severity. If our problem is patience, how regularly are we losing our patience? Moreover, when we do lose it, how long is it taking for us to calm back down? A few minutes? A few hours? A few days? Finally, when we lose it, to what extent are we doing so? Are we just feeling mental agitation or are we going one step further and expressing our frustration verbally—worse yet, physically? One of the many advantages of having a *mahātmā* like Amma in our lives is that we constantly have before us a living example of the pinnacle of *ātma-jñānam* and its manifestation. This is very helpful. At the same time, while holding the ideal of "Amma-hood" as our ultimate goal, on a daily basis Amma is not with whom we should judge our progress; we should judge our progress only by comparing ourselves with ourselves. If we constantly evaluate ourselves using Amma as the measuring stick, we may quickly become frustrated, decide we are spiritual failures and give up. However, if we use ourselves as our measuring stick—that is, if we judge our progress as Amma suggests on a day-to-day, week-to-week, year-to-year basis, analyzing it in terms of regularity, length and severity—the result will not be one of frustration but one of inspiration. As Amma says, "Let's say in the beginning, our goal is to remain patient in a trying circumstance just once a day. Even if we are only able to do this, say, five times a month, it is a great victory. You may not think so, but it is."

Thus, as we have seen, studying the characteristics of the *ātma-jñānī* presented in these sections of the Gītā has many benefits. Investigating their connection with *ātma-jñānam* helps us gain insight into the nature of self-knowledge itself—our life's goal. It provides an opportunity for us to make ourselves more aware of the values we need to cultivate in order to prepare the mind for self-knowledge. Moreover, it assists in evaluating our spiritual progress—the extent to which we have assimilated the spiritual teachings we are receiving from the scriptures and Amma.

THE CHARACTERISTICS OF THE SUPREME DEVOTEE

In this book, we will investigate one of the above-mentioned sections of the Gītā describing the characteristics of the *ātma-jñānī*, specifically the one found in the 12th chapter. There, from verse 13 through 19, Śrī Kṛṣṇa presents us with what is referred to as the *parābhakta lakṣaṇāni*—the characteristics of the supreme devotee. Together with the chapter's concluding 20th verse, this section is sometimes referred to as the Amṛtāṣṭakam. *Amṛta* means both nectar and immortal.[1] An *aṣṭakam* is a poem comprising eight verses. These eight verses have come to be known as the Amṛtāṣṭakam because of their concluding verse in which Kṛṣṇa refers to the qualities enumerated within them as *dharmyāmṛtam*, which means "the dharma that leads to immortality."

Before we begin our analysis of the Amṛtāṣṭakam, it is important that we understand why Kṛṣṇa's conviction is that, amongst all types of devotees, the *ātma-jñānī* stands supreme—a statement Kṛṣṇa has emphatically voiced in the Gītā's seventh chapter:

> caturvidhā bhajante māṁ janāḥ sukṛtino'rjuna |
> ārto jijñāsurarthārthī jñānī ca bharatarṣabha ||

[1] In the Purāṇas, there are many references to a type of sought-after nectar called amṛtam that bestows immortality. In fact, amṛtam is a symbol for the knowledge of the Vedas. The ritualistic section of the Vedas helps one attain a relative immortality through heaven, and the Upaniṣads bring one the understanding that he is, always has been, and always will be immortal.

teṣāṁ jñānī nitya-yukta eka-bhaktirviśiṣyate |
priyo hi jñānino'tyartham-ahaṁ sa ca mama priyaḥ ||

O Arjuna, best of Bharatas, four types of virtuous people worship me: the *ārta*, the *jijñāsu*, the *arthārthī* and the *jñānī*. Of these, the *jñānī*—ever-established and of one-pointed devotion—is superior. For, I am extremely dear to the *jñānī*, and he is extremely dear to me.[1]

In these two verses, Kṛṣṇa has divided devotees into four categories, using four technical names: *ārta*, *arthārthī*, *jijñāsu* and *jñānī*. The *ārta* devotee is one whose worship of God is aimed at removing him from some form of material difficulty—perhaps an illness, a lawsuit or a physical assault. The *arthārthī* devotee is one worshipping God as a means to attain various material gains—perhaps a promotion, a spouse, a winning lottery ticket, etc. The *jijñāsu* devotee is one who has come to understand that true, lasting happiness can never be achieved through avoiding material peril or fulfilling material desires, but only through attaining God. With this conviction, he has become a spiritual seeker. His worship and spiritual practices are, therefore, only aimed at bringing him closer to the Divine. *Jñānī*, of course, means *ātma-jñānī*: a knower of the self who has fully understood the truth that his true nature and the true nature of God are one and the same.

Why then does Kṛṣṇa say that of these four the *ātma-jñānī* is supreme? One can analyze this from a number of different angles, but the easiest reason to understand is revealed by Kṛṣṇa's description of the *jñānī* in the same verse: *nitya-yuktaḥ* and *eka-bhaktiḥ*. A *nitya-yuktaḥ* is one who is constantly established, unwavering. An *eka-bhaktiḥ* is one who has one-pointed devotion. Thus, according to Kṛṣṇa, the devotion of the *jñānī* is exemplary because it is the only devotion that is constant and one-pointed. With the first two types of devotion—the devotions of the *ārta* and *arthārthī* devotees—this is not the case. First of all, God is not really the object of their devotion, but merely the means to fulfill their material desires. Furthermore, their so-called devotion is, at best, divided three ways: between their

[1] Bhagavad-Gītā, 7.16-17

love for themselves, their love for their desired object, and their love for God, the means. Moreover, even their worship of God as a means continues only until their desire is fulfilled. Then it stops until another desire arises. Thus, their devotion can neither be called one-pointed nor unwavering.

The devotion of the *jijñāsu* is more mature. Perhaps, at its peak, it could even be called unwavering, but it cannot be called one-pointed. Why? Because the spiritual seeker is just what his name implies—a seeker. He has yet to fully understand and assimilate the truth that God and he are not two but one—that the seeker is, in fact, the sought. As Amma says, devotion is really just another word for love. It is out of his love for God and his desire to become one with God that the *jijñāsu* prays, does spiritual practices and studies the scriptures. However, because he has yet to understand that God and he are one—that God is, in fact, his true nature—his love cannot be called one-pointed. It remains divided between himself and God. Serving as Amma's translator during *darśan*, I often hear devotees telling Amma that they love her. When they say this, Amma sometimes takes the opportunity to shed some wisdom along these lines. She will say, "No. Not, 'I love you,' but 'I am love.' Remove the 'I' and the 'you,' and you will find that there is only 'love.' Until then, love remains imprisoned between the 'I' and the 'you.'" When Amma says this, she is illustrating the same point: Until we realize our unity with God, our devotion, or love, will not be supreme.

Now that we understand the defects in the other three forms of devotion, it is easy to understand why Kṛṣṇa says the *ātma-jñānī*'s love is unwavering and one-pointed and, therefore, superior. In essence, the reason is that the *ātma-jñānī* has understood the truth that he and God are one, and as a result of that understanding, he has become emotionally full and complete. He is, as Kṛṣṇa says in the second chapter, *ātmanyevātmanā tuṣṭaḥ*—"content in the self and by the self alone."[1] His love is one-pointed on God because he has no desires—nothing to pray for, nothing to seek. He does not want anything from

[1] Bhagavad-Gītā, 2.55

God. Knowing he is one with God, he doesn't even seek God. His constant self-experience is one of God, and everything he sees around him he knows to be merely an extension of his own self.

His understanding that he is one with God is also the reason why his love for God is unwavering. If we are honest there is only one person and one person alone for whom we have eternal, undying, unwavering love, and that is we ourselves. In fact, all our other so-called "beloveds" are subsidiary to this one primary love.

Recently, in Amritapuri, Amma was discussing selfless service with the residents, when she made a thought-provoking statement. She said, "Whatever I am doing, I am doing for myself." Was Amma saying she was selfish? She then explained, "My belief is that everyone in the world is my child. In fact, I don't see them as different from me. So, whatever I am doing, I am doing for myself." In essence, Amma was saying that truly selfless action is only possible when we see others as our own self. So, yes, Amma was saying that she was selfish—just that her self-conception was the entire universe.

In fact, the truth expressed here by Amma will be one of the central themes running through our investigation of the Amṛtāṣṭakam. For, as we will see, this understanding not only makes the *ātma-jñānī* the supreme devotee, it also gives rise to many of the divine qualities enumerated by Śrī Kṛṣṇa throughout these enlightening verses of the Gītā.

That said, with Amma's grace, let us commence our investigation into the Amṛtāṣṭakam.

Śrī Ādi Śaṅkarācārya

The guru-disciple lineages of India are like *mālās* strung with gems; each jewel is precious and invaluable. Still, some shine with an attention-commanding splendor. Śrī Ādi Śaṅkarācārya was such a diamond. His accomplishments were many, but he is singled out because his brilliant commentaries on the *prasthāna-trayam*—the Upaniṣads, Bhagavad-Gītā and Brahma Sūtras—crystallized the theology known as Advaita Vedānta, forever establishing it as the ultimate message of the Vedas. Śrī Śaṅkara did not invent Advaita Vedānta. Nor was he the first to write an Advaitic commentary upon the scriptures. However, such was the clarity and precision of his scriptural analysis and so profound its effect upon spiritual thought, that it remains today—nearly 2,000 years later—the foundational commentary for all modern Advaita Vedānta discussion. Throughout this book, we will often look to Śrī Śaṅkara's insights in order to shed light upon the Amṛtāṣṭakam. Therefore, at the outset, I would like to offer my heartfelt prostrations to Śrī Ādi Śaṅkarācārya and to the eternal guru-disciple lineage, before and after him, through which the Vedāntic knowledge has flowed down from time immemorial.

Amṛtāṣṭakam

adveṣṭā sarva-bhūtānām maitraḥ karuṇa eva ca |
nirmamo nirahaṅkāraḥ sama-duḥkha-sukhaḥ kṣamī ||

santuṣṭaḥ satataṁ yogī yatātmā dṛḍha-niścayaḥ |
mayyarpita-mano-buddhiryo mad-bhaktaḥ sa me priyaḥ ||

yasmānnodvijate loko lokānnodvijate ca yaḥ |
harṣāmarṣa-bhayodvegairmukto yaḥ sa ca me priyaḥ ||

anapekṣaḥ śucirdakṣa udāsīno gatavyathaḥ |
sarvārambha-parityāgī yo mad-bhaktaḥ sa me priyaḥ ||

yo na hṛṣyati na dveṣṭi na śocati na kāṅkṣati |
śubhāśubha-parityāgī bhaktimān yaḥ sa me priyaḥ ||

samaḥ śatrau ca mitre ca tathā manāpamānayoḥ |
śītoṣṇa-sukha-duḥkheṣu samaḥ saṅga-vivarjitaḥ ||

tulya-nindā-stutirmaunī santuṣṭo yena kenacit |
aniketaḥ sthiramatirbhaktimān-me priyo naraḥ ||

ye tu dharmyāmṛtam-idaṁ yathoktaṁ paryupāsate |
śraddadhānā mat-paramā bhaktāste'tīva me priyāḥ ||

He who is not hateful to any being, friendly, compassionate, devoid of "mine" and "I," who is the same in hardship and comfort, forgiving;

ever content, a yogī, self-controlled, of firm conviction, whose mind and intellect are fixed on me—such a devotee of mine is dear to me.

He who from the world cowers not and from whom the world doesn't cower, who is free of elation, impatience, fear and anxiety—he is dear to me.

The one devoid of desire, who is pure, efficient, impartial, free of affliction, a renouncer of all actions—such a devotee of mine is dear to me.

That devotee who doesn't elate, feel aversion, grief or desire, a renouncer of the auspicious and inauspicious—he is dear to me.

One who is the same toward enemy and friend, honor and dishonor, cold and heat, comfort and hardship, who is free of attachment;

who is the same in censure and praise, who is silent, content with anything, homeless, and firm in knowledge—that devotee is dear to me.

However, those who follow this above-said immortal dharma with faith, with me as the supreme goal—those devotees are [also] very dear to me.

One Who Hates No Being

SARVA-BHŪTĀNĀM ADVEṢṬĀ

The first description of the *parābhakta*[1] mentioned by Śrī Kṛṣṇa is *sarva-bhūtānām adveṣṭā*—one who harbors no feeling of hatred for any being. This is a statement made by Kṛṣṇa about the *ātma-jñānī*. He cannot hate; hatred is impossible for him.

In this regard, I remember an incident that took place in 2000. That year, a huge match-fixing scandal erupted in international cricket, making headlines throughout the world. It began when a phone conversation between the captain for South Africa and an Indian bookie was intercepted by Delhi police. In the conversation, the captain spoke explicitly about his willingness to lose games intentionally in exchange for money. An official inquiry soon followed. The captain ultimately admitted to wrongdoing and was given a lifetime ban from cricket. During the inquiry, he implicated other players, including two who played for India. Soon, they were also given bans, along with several others associated with India's team.

In India, cricket is like a national religion. For example, in 2011, when India went to the World Cup, it was reported that 67.6 million people in India watched the final game. Part of the reason for this is that the team is not a city team, but a national team, with the entire nation rooting for it. So, in 2000, when the two India players were revealed to have intentionally tried to lose games, the nation was livid. The country's sentiment was, "How dare these people, who already made so much money, betray the nation that loved them—and that they also supposedly loved back—for a few pieces of silver?"

While they don't get many opportunities to watch matches, there are a few *āśram* residents who remain cricket fans and continue to follow the team's standings, etc, in the newspaper. One of them soon

---

[1] As mentioned in the Introduction, parābhakta means "one with supreme devotion." Although we typically think of a devotee in dualistic terms, it is Kṛṣṇa's view that only one with self-knowledge can truly be called a supreme devotee, since only the ātma-jñānī sees God as non-different from his own self, etc.

found himself discussing some matters with Amma, but while he was talking to Amma, his mind kept returning to the scandal and how the implicated Indian players had betrayed their team and their nation. Finally, when a break in the conversation arose, he managed to mention the issue. He told Amma everything that had happened. Amma listened intently, seemingly encouraging the young man to share his heart, including all his various judgments against the now-banned players.

Typically when we share our feelings with someone, it is because we want them to agree with us, to share in our feelings. This is because if it is a joyous experience, we can prolong our experience of joy through sharing it and, if it is a negative experience, we can, to some extent, curtail our anger and sorrow through others accepting our justifications. As the saying goes, "Shared joy is double joy; shared sorrow is half sorrow." Amma listened intently as he explained the scandal, allowing him to vent his feelings. At the same time she was aware that what he really wanted was for Amma to express enmity as well. At the peak of his tirade, he suddenly noticed that instead of the scowl he was subconsciously hoping to see forming on Amma's face, there was just a soft smile. Something about this silenced him. At which point, Amma said, "Son, you know Amma cannot hate anyone–don't you?"

The *ātma-jñānī* simply cannot hate; it has been stripped from his mental programming. In his commentary on the Gītā verse in which this quality is mentioned, Ādi Śaṅkarācārya elaborates a bit further, writing:

> He does not feel hatred for anything, even for that which is [typically considered] a cause of sorrow, for he sees all beings as his own self.[1]

Śrī Śaṅkara reveals the depth of this quality in the *ātma-jñānī*. It is not only that he doesn't feel hatred in a general sense, but even when someone harms him–verbally or physically–the emotion does not arise.

---

[1] na dveṣṭā ātmano duḥkha-hetum api na kiṁcid dveṣṭi sarvāṇi bhūtāni ātmatvena hi paśyati |

I have personally witnessed Amma's inability to hate countless times. When I first started coming to Amma in the late 1970s, there was a group of atheistic villagers who were dead set against Amma. They wanted to expose her as a fake, and when they continually failed to do so, they took it upon themselves to try everything they could to harass the devotees, Amma's family, Amma's disciples and even Amma herself. They strew poisonous thorns on Amma's pathway, gave Amma poisoned milk, fabricated lies about her and inflicted upon her many cruelties. Yet, I never saw Amma become angry with them. I never heard Amma curse them. I never saw Amma take any form of revenge. Myself and the other *brahmacārīs* would become very angry. Of course, like the young man who told Amma about the deplorable deeds of the match-fixers, what we really wanted was to rile Amma up as well. However, to our chagrin, Amma would never play along. She would just softly smile and say, "Son, they are ignorant. We should be patient with them."

Over the years the majority of the people who were harassing Amma and the Āśram back then have become devotees. (In fact, one of them even went on to marry Amma's elder sister.) However, that doesn't mean that the Āśram no longer faces obstacles and occasional opposition. In such circumstances—although by now it shouldn't—Amma's inability to feel enmity never ceases to astound me.

For example, about 10 years ago, someone wrote a negative article about an Āśram project in one of the Malayalam newspapers. It was full of twisted truths and outright lies. Everyone knew that the writer was a puppet of an antireligious organization, but that didn't make the article sting any less. The other *āśram* residents and I were very angry. Regardless of how much I tried to convince Amma how hate-deserving this particular journalist was, she wasn't giving in.

About a year later, the same writer suddenly came for Amma's *darśan*. Someone pointed him out to me, and I quickly made my way to Amma's side so that I could point him out to her. When I did so, Amma said, "Son, I know very well who he is. In fact, I think he's probably here to cause more trouble." As he came closer and closer to Amma in the *darśan* line, I wondered what Amma was going to say to him. (At the same time, I was also imagining all the things that I would say if he were coming for my *darśan*.) Finally it was the reporter's turn. What did Amma do? Amma took him into her arms just like everyone else and gave him a very long, very beautiful *darśan*, the whole time calling him her darling, darling son. There's nothing we can do about it: Amma cannot hate.

As I watched the man leave the stage with Amma's *prasādam* clutched in his hand, I shook my head once again in disbelief at Amma's compassion. I realized that, as unrighteous as the man's deeds had been, Amma understood that calling this person out and scolding him would not have uplifted him. It would only have served to further close his heart. Amma knew that only by returning the journalist's cruelty with love could she truly hope to affect a change within him.

As mentioned in the Introduction, the full blossoming of qualities such as non-hatred is only found in the *ātma-jñānī* because their full manifestation can only come as a result of self-knowledge. We have to try to inculcate non-hatred as an ideal in order to prepare our mind for self-knowledge, but its full expression only comes as a fruit of that knowledge.

There are a number of reasons why non-hatred is produced by *ātma-jñānam*. We will look at two. The first reason is presented by Śrī Śaṅkara himself as quoted previously. Śrī Śaṅkara writes that the *ātma-jñānī* cannot hate any being because he sees all beings as his own self.

The scriptures and spiritual masters inform us repeatedly that we are not the body, not the emotions, not the intellect, but the witness consciousness that serves as the substratum to these and all other varieties of phenomena. Furthermore, we are told that this consciousness is not only our true nature but also the nature of all beings. Consciousness, we are told, is like space. The space outside a given room and the space within it are not two; they are one and the same. Similarly, the consciousness serving as the substratum of my thoughts and emotions, etc, is not different than the consciousness serving as the substratum of your thoughts and emotions, etc. By extension of this understanding, we should come to the reality that—quite literally—"I am you and you are me." It is the assimilation of this supreme truth that results in the *ātma-jñānī*'s inability to experience hatred. This is because it is a common experience that one cannot hate one's self.

As Amma says, "A spiritual aspirant should see only God, which is the essence in everything. Only then will he achieve equanimity. The electricity that comes through a fan, bulb or refrigerator is one and the same. The only difference is in the medium. Likewise, it is the same consciousness that dwells in all living beings. We will not feel hatred or anger toward anyone when we think that the consciousness that dwells in him is the same as in me."

Nowhere has this connection been expressed more directly than in the Upaniṣads:

> yastu sarvāṇi bhūtānyātmanyevānupaśyati |
> sarva-bhūteṣu cātāmānaṁ tato na vijugupsate ||
>
> He who sees all beings in the self itself, and the self in all beings, feels no hatred by virtue of that.[1]

Some may disagree with the statement that we cannot hate ourselves. In fact, it is a common expression, "I hate myself so much right now." Some people even commit suicide—perpetrating the ultimate form of violence upon their own being. So, how can Vedānta make such a claim?

When someone says, "I hate myself," if we analyze, we will see that he doesn't really mean what he is saying. He may mean he hates his physical body. He may mean he hates the actions he has performed, his habits or the direction his life is taking. He could even mean he hates his thoughts and feelings. However, as the scriptures and spiritual gurus like Amma repeatedly tell us, these things are not who we are. In fact, this points to the very difference between the self-enlightened individual and the self-ignorant. The self-ignorant mistakes himself to be things he is not: the body, emotions and intellect. Thus he believes he hates himself. True introspection will reveal that the very statement

[1] Īśāvāsya Upaniṣad, 6

"I hate myself," is, in fact, not an expression of self-hatred but an expression of self-love. For the very reason a person comes to hate his body, emotions and intellect is that he wants to experience peace and happiness, which are his true nature. He wants to reside in his true nature. This experience is being obscured to him due to his turbulent mind. Thus, self-hatred and even the desire to end one's life have at their root the desire to know and experience the bliss and peace of one's true self. If the hated factor could be changed, the individual's so-called "self-hatred" would end. Of course, suicide is not a solution to this problem because at the problem's root are mental phenomena, which the scriptures say can never be eradicated by death.[1] The only solution is gradual refinement of one's thoughts and the ultimate transcendence of mental identification—in short, spirituality.

In order to understand the second reason why self-knowledge results in non-hatred, we first have to understand an important Vedāntic principle. If we honestly introspect, we will see that we are only capable of loving two things: the experience of happiness itself and the people, places and things, etc, that serve as a means to our experience of happiness. When we study the scriptures, we find that, in fact, there is only one source for our experience of happiness, and that is the *ātmā*—our true self. The *ātmā* is often explained as *sat cit ānanda*—being of the nature of pure existence, pure consciousness and pure bliss. Thus, happiness is our true nature; it is the core of who we are. No wonder we love happiness so much: our love of happiness is the same as our love of our own self. The scriptures are adamant on this point: the self is the only source of happiness in this universe. So, why then does it seem like we are experiencing happiness from, for example, ice cream? The scriptures explain to us that, in fact, our desire for such objects is creating turbulence in the

---

[1] According to the Vedas, only the physical body dies upon death. The subtle body—the locus of the mind and its emotional problems and negativities—survives and is eventually reborn in another physical frame. Thus, Amma says that if one commits suicide, not only will they have to face the same difficulties again in a future birth but those very difficulties will be intensified as an effect of the violence they have committed against themselves.

mind, which in turn is obscuring our experience of our true nature. When our desires are fulfilled, this turbulence momentarily dissipates to some small degree, and to the same degree the bliss of the self is then momentarily reflected in the mind for our experience. Thus, the experience of happiness is not coming from the experience of the external object but from the self. The object is merely a means for temporarily removing the desire-created turbulence obscuring our experience of the self as reflected in our mind.

Through this principle, we can now understand another reason why the *ātma-jñānī* is incapable of hatred. For just as we are only capable of loving two things—the experience of happiness itself, and people, places and things, etc, that we believe serve as a means to the experience of happiness—similarly, we are only capable of hating two things: the non-experience of happiness, and people, places and things, etc, that we believe obstruct our experience of happiness. However, the *ātma-jñānī* has understood happiness to have only one source—himself. This is not only his understanding; he has assimilated this truth to the point where he no longer has desire-created turbulence disturbing his mind and obstructing his experience of the reflection of the self. Thus, his experience of happiness is no longer dependent upon "middlemen" such as ice cream. Therefore, neither can anyone remove the *ātma-jñānī*'s experience of happiness, nor can anyone give the *ātma-jñānī* the experience of happiness. If we are only capable of hating the non-experience of happiness, and people, places and things, etc, that prevent our experience of happiness, what scope is there for hatred in the *ātma-jñānī*?

In the sixth chapter of the Gītā, there is an oft-cited verse, wherein Śrī Kṛṣṇa points out the Vedāntic truth that one has only one enemy—one's own mind when it is undisciplined and lacking in spiritual understanding:

> uddhared-ātmanātmānaṁ nātmānam-avasādayet |
> ātmaiva hyātmano bandhurātmaiva ripūrātmanaḥ ||

> One should uplift oneself by oneself; one should not lower oneself. For oneself alone is one's friend and oneself alone is one's enemy.[1]

In his commentary, Śrī Śaṅkara expresses a possible doubt regarding this statement. In resolving that doubt he sheds light on why an *ātma-jñānī* cannot hate any being. The doubt is: How can Kṛṣṇa say, "Oneself *alone* is one's enemy. While a mind in which negativities are manifesting can be counted as one internal enemy, it does not preclude the existence of additional external enemies." Śrī Śaṅkara answers, saying, "Whoever may be an external enemy is also of his own making alone. Therefore the emphatic 'alone' is logical."[2] A brilliant post-Śaṅkara commentator[3] elucidates Śrī Śaṅkara's logic. He says that if one has truly understood spirituality (as the *ātma-jñānī*, by his very name, has), then he knows that he is not the body-mind but the *ātmā*—pure consciousness. The very scope for considering someone as an enemy arises only from identification with the body-mind complex and the feelings of "I" and "mine," the byproducts of that identification. An *ātma-jñānī* has transcended this false identification and thus has only one potential enemy—the self-misconception itself. Without the rising of that misconception, there is no scope for an external enemy.

As mentioned in the Introduction, if we want to cultivate total non-hatred, we must understand these connections. Our understanding of who we are must be redirected from our current distorted misconception to our true self. This understanding cannot be superficial. It has to saturate our subconscious mind; it has to come to serve not as a mere piece of information but to reform our entire self-conception and worldview. This process of *ātma-jñānam* converting from mere information to a hardwired transformation in self-conception takes time. In the beginning, we may understand intellectually that, for example, the consciousness at the heart of who we are and the consciousness at the heart of all beings is one and the

---

1 Gītā, 6.5

2 yaḥ anyaḥ apakārī bāhyaḥ śatruḥ saḥ api ātma-prayukta eva iti yuktam eva avadhāraṇam

3 Śrī Bellaṅkoṇḍa Rāmarāya Kavī (1875–1914), Gitā-Bhāṣyārka-Prakāśika

same, yet hatred and other thoughts contrary to this understanding will still arise. The Vedāntic term for this phenomenon is *viparīta bhāvanā*, which literally means "contrary attitude." In essence, it means the arising of thoughts from the subconscious that are contrary to one's conscious understanding. It is a thought arising from habit, instead of from knowledge.

When speaking of *viparīta bhāvanā*, Amma always gives the example of a wristwatch. She says, "Suppose we have a wristwatch that we wear all the time. It is always on the wrist, but one day we sell it. For a few days afterward, we will continue to look at our wrist to see the time. This is the nature of habit. If this is the case with ordinary and seemingly insignificant habits, what to say of the stronger ones? When we try to change them, our mind will spontaneously turn again and again toward our habits. Only through constant practice can one get rid of them."

There is no stronger habit than our identification with the body, emotions and intellect. To remove it takes constant effort and practice. It is not easy. I remember when I was a *brahmacārī*, Amma would tell me never to express anger, but only to say *namaśśivaya*[1] and walk away. However, my anger was so intense that—if at all I managed to succeed in this—the anger would still manifest in my intonation. When such negative feelings arise, as sincere seekers, we must check ourselves and remind ourselves of the supreme truth of our essential oneness with all beings. For the very arising of hatred is proof that we have forgotten this truth. This must be done each and every time such feelings arise. In this way, we can gradually rewire our subconscious mind until it conforms to our new understanding of who we are. Not only should we do this in our daily lives, we should also make this practice part of our morning and evening meditations. There, with our calmed mind, we should remember the situations that are prompting our negative reactions. Then we should uproot the sources of those reactions by remembering the spiritual truths that negate them, affirming and appreciating the reality of those truths.

[1] "Prostrations to Śiva," which has diverse meanings including pure consciousness, auspiciousness and God.

A Friend

MAITRAḤ

The next description of the *parābhakta* given by Śrī Kṛṣṇa is *maitraḥ*—a friend. It is no coincidence that this quality immediately follows non-hatred in Kṛṣṇa's list. If Kṛṣṇa were to mention only non-hatred, we might get the wrong impression: that the *ātma-jñānī* is an aloof figure, not hating anyone but also not expressing any positive affection either. This is a prevalent misconception about spirituality—that it transforms the seeker into a recluse who doesn't hate anyone but who doesn't really care about anyone either. By saying he is a friend, Kṛṣṇa wants to end this misconception.

In today's world, the word "friend" is used quite casually. However, we all know that there are different levels of friendship. The friendship of the *ātma-jñānī* is not superficial. It is a friendship that is always there for us—not only in our joy but also in our sorrow. It is a friendship that never expects anything in return and that would gladly sacrifice everything for our happiness. A popular American children's book, *The Giving Tree* by Shel Silverstein, provides an excellent example.[1] The tree in the book cheerfully gives everything, without any regrets, to her friend, the boy. She verily lives for the boy. She allows him to play and swing from her branches when he is a child. She allows him to sell her apples when he wants money as a teenager. She allows him to cut down her branches and use them to build a house when he is a man. She even allows him to chop her down entirely and make a boat out of her trunk upon his retirement. Finally, when the man is old and infirm and can barely even walk anymore, the Giving Tree allows him to simply sit on her stump. The Giving Tree never asked for anything in return. Such is the level of friendship found in the *ātma-jñānī*.

It is important to note that Kṛṣṇa says that the *ātma-jñānī* is not only a friend to a few select individuals, but that his feeling of

---

[1] Shel Silverstein, *The Giving Tree*, Harper & Row, 1964.

friendship extends to *sarva-bhūtānām*—to all beings.[1] What better example of such a person do we have than Amma? No matter where she goes, no matter who she meets, no matter how old or how young, how traditional or how modern, how serious, or how silly, how rich or poor, educated or otherwise, no matter what language they speak, Amma feels totally comfortable and at home with them and treats them with warmth, kindness, love and affection. This is one of the many ways in which Amma truly is an *amma*—a mother. It is Amma's friendliness that draws many of us close to her, helping us to establish that all-important bond that ultimately helps us to transcend all bondage.

When Amma is giving programs throughout India, she will occasionally stop at the houses of devotees. Once Amma was at one such house, spending time talking with the family. Suddenly, the youngest child—who was about 17 at the time—began telling Amma about the devotion of her older sister. She told Amma how she would often see her sister shedding tears while listening to Amma singing. Amma is a brilliant psychologist. If there is a subtext, a hidden meaning behind a statement, Amma will see it. As such, when this girl told Amma about her sister's devotion, Amma knew the real statement was not "My sister cries whenever she hears *bhajans*," but rather "I never cry when I listen to *bhajans*. What's wrong with me? Why don't I have any spiritual longing? Don't I even have one spiritual bone in my body?" Thus, Amma the psychologist responded, not to the gross statement, but to the hidden one. Amma told the girl, "But you and I are friends, aren't we? We share a friendship. There is only love between us. Devotion means to evoke the love within you. Amma doesn't see devotion and love as different from each other." With wonder in her eyes, the girl smiled at Amma and said, "You're right."

The love and kinship Amma feels with all beings reflects in our hearts, and it helps us to open up to Amma as well.

When Kṛṣṇa says "a friend to all beings," he doesn't just mean all types of people. The heart of the *ātma-jñānī* extends with the feeling of

[1] Sarva-bhūtānām not only modifies non-hatred but also friendship.

friendship to every aspect of creation. Amma's biography is filled with stories illustrating the reciprocal heartfelt bond between Amma and various animals, and I have personally seen Amma give *darśan* not just to common pets like cats and dogs, but also to parrots, eagles, horses, wolves, cows, goats, camels, beetles, owls, rabbits, chipmunks, bats, turtles, pythons, boa constrictors, monkeys, cheetahs, and elephants. Amma's heart truly has a space for every aspect of creation. It never ceases to amaze me how she never forgets to consider the needs and feelings of even those creatures we typically think of as insignificant.

I remember, one day an *āśram* resident offered Amma a flower garland, placing it around her neck as he came for *darśan*. The flowers seemed particularly beautiful to me, and I said as much to Amma. Amma smiled and said, "Yes, but don't you think it is sad that someone plucked them before their time? And what of the poor bees who were hoping to sip nectar from them today? Amma is happy with any offering her children make, but I am not only a mother to them. Aren't the flowers and bees also my children?" I was really taken aback by the expansiveness of Amma's vision.[1]

Exactly why is it that the heart of the *ātma-jñānī* flows out to all of creation with a feeling of friendship? Here, too, there are a number of different reasons depending upon the angle taken. Spiritually ignorant individuals are totally identified with their likes and dislikes. When we identify with our likes and dislikes, they restrict with whom we are capable of feeling a heartfelt bond. Thus, our friendships are limited to like-minded people. Due to his self-understanding, the *ātma-jñānī* no longer identifies with such mental phenomena. For him, likes and dislikes are no different than clouds passing across the changeless all-pervasive sky of consciousness. Thus, he identifies with the consciousness that serves as their substratum, and this frees him to take up the likes and dislikes of the people who come before him. We see this in our interactions with Amma. When we come before

[1] As with many statements made by Amma, we have to understand the context in which this comment was made. This person was an āśram resident, and thus Amma was holding him to a higher standard. On other occasions Amma has specifically said that she has no issue with people offering flowers in temples, etc.

her, she becomes like a mirror reflecting our heart. This is how Amma can switch from total sorrow to total happiness in the blink of an eye. A devotee comes to Amma crying and tells of a family tragedy, and Amma identifies with him and cries along with him. A minute later, the next devotee excitedly announces to Amma that she graduated with honors, and we immediately see her joy radiating across Amma's face. Amma identifies with our likes and dislikes and the emotions they produce because she knows it provides us with the strength, sense of friendship and support that we need to move forward in life. She knows it strengthens the bond we feel with her and that through that bond she can guide us toward attainment of the higher goals of life. All this is only possible due to Amma's *ātma-jñānam* and how it allows her to transcend likes and dislikes.

Amma was born and brought up in a small Kerala fishing village. She was raised by parents with very traditional Indian values. Of course, these include universal values such as the ones mentioned by Kṛṣṇa in the Gītā, but they also include values specific to traditional Indian villages. Not all devotees were raised with the culture-specific values with which Amma was brought up. Regardless, we never see Amma trying to convince people from other cultures to try to follow those culture-specific values. Amma accepts those culture-specific values or discards them depending upon the person whom she is advising. As Amma says, "Some things, like the sweetness of sugar or the value of gold, are the same wherever one goes, but other things, such as whether one drives on the left or right side of the road, change from place to place. In this regard every place has its own unique culture." It is difficult for someone completely identified with their culture-specific values to become close friends with those who do not share those values. However, for Amma, this has never been a problem. When she is in Germany, she adjusts to the German culture. When in Japan, to theirs. So, too, in America, Australia, Kenya... Amma's self-knowledge has freed her to accept and reject the superficial according to the given situation, and this allows Amma to make a heartfelt connection with anyone and everyone no matter what their likes and dislikes may be.

Let me give you an example. A few years ago a teenaged Indian boy born and raised in America came for Amma's *darśan.* As per the culture of many teenagers in America, he had recently got his ears pierced and had a small silver hoop in each ear. The boy's mother was clearly unhappy. Being from another generation, and raised in a traditional Indian environment, she didn't want her teenaged son wearing earrings. In truth, according to the culturally specific values with which Amma was raised, earrings are not something generally worn by men either. However, knowing these values were not pertinent to the boy, who was raised in America, Amma rejected them and took up the values of the boy. When Amma saw the earrings, she said, "Oh, they look so nice! But wouldn't it look better if you got some slightly bigger ones?" In fact, this was what the boy really wanted all along. While Amma will never accept a culturally specific value that goes against the universal values, she adjusts to values such as these as per the cultural norm of the person who comes before her.

This is one reason why *ātma-jñānam* results in one becoming a friend with all beings: it ceases our identification with our likes and dislikes and liberates us to take up the likes and dislikes of the people with whom we interact.

In fact, friendship is the natural mood of humanity. It is an outward expression of the bliss that is our true nature. Thus, for the *ātma-jñānī*, this attitude flows forth, as natural as breathing. The expression is blocked only by the fear that arises when we perceive something as having the potential to obstruct our experience of inner bliss. This is never an issue for the *ātma-jñānī* because he has realized that there is only one source of bliss—his own self. Thus, no one can possibly obstruct it. Can anyone obstruct you from experiencing your self? There is no fear in him that, "Oh, this fellow walking in my direction can take away my happiness." Thus, the sense of aversion, which is the very thing that obstructs the experience of happiness, never arises in his mind. Let the most annoying person in the world come pester him, his happiness continues to shine.

This phenomenon is quite fascinating. In our spiritual ignorance, we project the capability to destroy our happiness upon someone who actually holds no such power to do so. However, through this projection, we actually bestow upon him that power. It is similar to the phenomenon of a bank run, wherein people become afraid that, if everyone tries to withdraw their money from the bank at the same time, the bank will fold and they will lose their money, which in turn causes everyone to try to withdraw their money and results in the bank folding. Or we can compare it to the phenomenon of stage fright, wherein, say, a violinist, realizes that if he gets nervous and his hands start shaking he will not be able to perform. This very thought, in turn, makes him so nervous that his hands shake and he cannot perform. In reality, no one has the power to stop our experience of the bliss of the self. We project that power upon their presence. Then, the sight of them approaching results in mental disturbance in the form of aversion, which does obstruct our experience of bliss. Thus, it truly is as the saying goes, "The only thing we have to fear is fear itself."

Those of us who have yet to attain self-knowledge are constantly subconsciously evaluating people as either potential causes of happiness or potential causes of suffering. The people we see as vectors of happiness, we are attracted to and we consider our friends. The people we see as vectors of sorrow, we feel aversion toward and consider as enemies. The *ātma-jñānī* does not live in such a world. He is not imprisoned by likes and dislikes like the rest of us. He has understood that happiness only comes from within, and thus he has severed the ignorance-based connection that most people believe exists between certain individuals and happiness and certain individuals and sorrow. Thus, friendliness, the natural expression of the bliss of the self, never ceases to flow forth from him to all of creation.

Becoming a friend to all beings to the extent that Amma has is not easy. In some ways, the first quality mentioned by Kṛṣṇa, non-hatred toward all beings, is level-one spirituality, and feeling friendship toward all beings is level two. An *āśram* resident once told me a story that reveals Amma's appreciation of this fact. He had just moved to Amritapuri and, as such, felt very inspired. When you witness firsthand the extent to which Amma is sacrificing herself, day-in and day-out, to help others, you cannot help but be inspired to try—in whatever small way possible—to move toward a life of selflessness like Amma's. This is how this individual felt. Thus, one day, he approached Amma and, with his heart open wide, told her that he also wanted to love everyone selflessly like she did. Amma looked at him with eyes full of compassion, gave him a loving peck on the cheek and sweetly said, "Son, to begin with, just try not to hate anyone."

Therefore, we should understand that feeling loving friendship toward everyone is not easy. Ultimately, it must be reinforced at a core level by regularly reminding ourselves of the Vedāntic truth of our essential unity. As mentioned in the previous chapter, this should be done both when our attitudes run contrary to this understanding, as well as in our daily focused meditations.

A Compassionate Person

KARUṆAḤ

The next quality of the *parābhakta* mentioned by Śrī Kṛṣṇa is *karuṇaḥ*—compassion. Not long ago, I read an article by a Christian theologian that gave a beautiful definition for mercy, which I think works fine for compassion: "The willingness to enter the chaos of another."[1] Like Amma, this definition transforms compassion from a mere emotion into an action. Amma often says that love is the inner feeling and compassion its outward expression—i.e. love in action. Like Amma, it also implies that compassion most often involves sacrifice. "Entering chaos" is not a casual experience. When people are suffering physically and emotionally, their lives are often messy. Family problems, financial problems, social problems, problems of mental and physical health—they all can create a very disturbing environment. The burden and pain they create in those suffering from them can result in tension, depression, frustration and anger. Just because we are trying to help the afflicted person doesn't mean that we won't become the target of these negative emotions. Thus, compassion is being there for someone and helping them despite all of that, sacrificing your time, energy and resources.

What is Amma's *darśan* but her entering the chaos of thousands upon thousands of lives? Each person coming in the queue to Amma is bringing with them their pain, their problems, their fears. Amma tangibly enters their lives, holding them in that heartfelt embrace, listening to their lamentations, drying their tears, often shedding tears herself. It is in Amma's life that we see compassion expressed in its totality. Amma constantly sacrifices food, sleep, solitude, rest—all the things we believe make life comfortable—simply to bring as many smiles to as many people as possible, to wipe as many tears as possible, to be there to unburden the sorrows of as many people

---

1 James F. Keenan, S.J., *Moral Wisdom: Lessons and Texts from the Catholic Tradition*, Sheed & Ward, 2010.

as possible. Why does Amma make this seeming sacrifice? Because Amma knows that in her arms people feel safe, feel comforted, feel that finally they've found someone who knows them through and through. With that feeling, they get the strength to move forward in life, and this, Amma feels, is infinitely more important than her physical comfort.

I would like to share an incident that illustrates the extent to which Amma, in her compassion, is willing to sacrifice for the world—how she is willing to give and give and give, even to her own physical detriment. This took place in 2006 when Amma was in Kannur, northern Kerala. It was an extremely large crowd. Amma had come for the program at 7:00 p.m. the evening before and, at 9:00 a.m. the next morning, was still giving *darśan*. At some point, early in the night, one of the devotees had asked Amma if, before she drove on to Bangalore, she would stop at his house. Amma had agreed. As the *darśan* was going so late, I couldn't believe his audacity. Amma had been sitting on the stage for 14 hours continuously without any food or rest. The next day would bring another large *darśan* in Bangalore, and, yet, this man was pushing Amma to come to his house. Amma assured him that she would come.

When the *darśan* finally finished, we learned that the man's house was completely out of the way. At this point, I was upset. I told myself that when we reached his house, I was going to explain to him that what he had requested of Amma was incorrect. After a half an hour or so, we arrived. Amma gracefully alighted from her camper and, looking as fresh as ever, entered the man's house. She did a simple *pūjā* in the *pūjā* room, and then the man asked Amma to go to yet another room. I couldn't believe it: it seemed it wasn't enough that Amma had come to his house; this man wanted Amma to enter and bless each and every room. Again, Amma gracefully agreed.

When we entered the room, I suddenly realized why Amma had agreed to come. There, on the bed, was his child who suffered from hydrocephalus. His legs and arms were like toothpicks, and his head was more than double the size of a normal head. It was so large that he could not even lift it without assistance, and even then, it was obviously very painful for him. There was no way he could have come to the program. Amma held the child, cradling his massive head in her arms and fed him with her own hands, whispering in his ear, "My *son... my son... my son...*" I felt so ashamed for my judgment of this devotee and admonished myself for second-guessing Amma and her deeper understanding of what is and isn't required.

The fact was that, physically, Amma had to have been exhausted. The *darśan* had gone on for 14 hours, and the next day's *darśan* would probably be just as long. There is no way that such physical strain doesn't have an effect on Amma's health, and there is no way that Amma is not aware of that. However, due to the enormity of Amma's compassion, there was only one fact that was relevant to Amma: "One of my children is alone and in pain, and I have the power to bring him at least a small amount of comfort."

How is Amma able to be like this? How is she able to give and give and give, even when that giving seems to be detrimental to her best interests? Why, as Kṛṣṇa says, is compassion a natural expression for an *ātma-jñānī*? Here, we must remember that a core teaching of Advaita Vedānta is that there is only one *ātmā*. The proponents of Advaita draw upon many scriptural statements attesting to this truth. One such statement comes in Svetāśvatara Upaniṣad:

> eko devaḥ sarvabhūteṣu guḍhaḥ sarvavyāpī sarva-bhūtāntarātmā |
>
> The one God, hidden in all beings, all-pervasive, the inner *ātmā* of all beings.[1]

Kṛṣṇa also says this in his own unique way, referring to all the various bodies as "fields" and the one *ātmā* as "the knower of all the fields":

> kṣetrajñaṁ cāpi mām viddhi sarva-kṣetreṣu bhārata |
>
> O Bhārata, also know me as the knower of the fields in all fields.[2]

[1] Śvetāśvatara Upaniṣad, 6.11

[2] Gītā, 13.2

Amma also has her own unique ways of expressing this truth as well: "All of us are different forms of the one *ātmā*, like chocolate [Hershey's Kisses] in different colored wrappers. The chocolate wrapped in a green wrapper may tell the chocolate wrapped in a red wrapper, 'I'm different from you,' and the chocolate wrapped in red paper may tell the chocolate in blue paper, 'You and I are different,' but once the wrappers are removed, all the chocolates are exactly the same. In the same way, at the heart of every one of us is the one and the same *ātmā*."

What these scriptural statements and Amma are telling us is that if we strip away the superficial layers of our being—the physical layer, the emotional layer, the intellectual layer, etc—what remains is the pure awareness, pure consciousness, the true "I." While the superficial layers are different, the true "I" is one and the same for every being.

If we are all one inside, why is that not our experience? Why do we feel separate? This is a common doubt. To understand this, it is helpful if we look at an example Amma frequently uses. She says, "Suppose you take 100 pots of water and put them out under the sun. In each pot, you will see a sun—won't you? But that doesn't mean there are 100 different suns. The sun is one; the reflections are many." Looking at Amma's example, the reason we fail to appreciate our oneness is that we are either identifying with the pot, the water in the pot or—at best—the reflection in the water in the pot. We are forgetting the original sun. In Amma's example, the various pots represent our physical bodies. At this level, some of us are big round pots, some tall skinny flute-like pots, some white, some brown, etc. The water in the various pots represents our individual minds—some of us have calm-water minds, some agitated-water minds, some muddy-water minds, some pure-water minds, etc. According to Vedānta, the sun reflected in each pot is getting closer to the permanent reality, but is still not our true nature. It is but a reflection of the *ātmā* in our mind, what some Vedānta scholars refer to as *cidābhāsa*—reflected consciousness. Our true nature is the sun—the original consciousness. The original consciousness is one and the same for all. It is not modified by the conditions of the reflecting medium of the mind/water. This is the true eternal nature of all of us. An *ātma-jñānī* like Amma roots his identity and the identity of every aspect of creation—sentient and insentient—in the original consciousness. They are able to discriminate themselves and others not only from the physical body and mind, but also from consciousness as reflected in the mind. Identifying with that true self, they see themselves in others and others in themselves.

It is our obsession with our differences that prevents us from appreciating our oneness. The *ātmā* is the ultimate reality of each of us—whole, complete and infinite. Beyond that shared and permanent reality, I will experience a certain set of finite, internal and external changing phenomena; you will experience a different set. Regardless, these temporary experiences have absolutely no bearing on the infinite shared reality of who we are—the original consciousness. As Swāmī Dayānanda Sarasvatī, a popular Vedānta teacher, said, we should consider our individual body, mind and senses as an addition to the whole, not a diminution.

The *jñānī*'s complete and total understanding of the oneness of the *ātmā* is the source of his compassion. We all love ourselves. We never get tired of feeding ourselves, of bathing ourselves, of striving to better ourselves, of comforting and indulging ourselves. When it comes to ourselves, it is a lifelong labor of love. Amma says that the *ātma-jñānī* has understood that his self does not end at the confines of his physical body but, in fact, pervades all bodies. He knows that the phenomenon of individuality is a mere illusion. This understanding has registered within him to such a depth that his response to the suffering of others is 100 percent in tune with that reality. It is, as Amma always says, "Suppose the left hand is injured. Does the right hand say, 'Oh, that's the left hand; it has nothing to do with me?' No, the right hand immediately presses and soothes the left hand, applies medicine if needed. This is because it does not see the left hand as different from itself. If we have true spiritual understanding, this is how we will react to the suffering of all beings."

I remember once in response to someone's question, Amma was explaining the nature of her *darśan*—why she just naturally embraces everyone and showers them with affection. She said, "It's just the outward flow of Amma's inherent compassion. That flow happens spontaneously when you come to Amma. Just as leaves flutter when the wind arrives, just as sweetness is the inherent nature of a fruit, the motherly sentiment, the flow of compassion, is Amma's inherent nature. What can Amma do? The feeling of oneness is very real to her. A cow may be black or white or red, but the milk is always white. Similarly, there is only one *ātmā*, not many. It only appears as many to those who think of themselves as the *jīvātmā*.[1] That's all there is to it. Amma doesn't feel that distinction." Thus, Amma has said very clearly that her compassion is a direct outcome of the fact that "the feeling of oneness is very real to her." It is Amma's *ātma-jñānam*—her knowledge that the self in her is the self in all beings. Her compassion is all-pervasive because her sense of self is all-pervasive.

Several years back someone showed me a short story that reflects this aspect of Amma.[2] The story is about a couple that finds an undernourished, abandoned puppy in their backyard. These are good people, and they feel the puppy is now—by whatever twist of fate—their responsibility. The puppy is cute enough, but they immediately realize it has a problem. In its thus-far short life it has been horribly mistreated. As a result, it barks constantly, and when anyone tries to offer it comfort, it whimpers, cowers with fear and urinates. It is simply terrified of anything and everything—especially humans.

Despite their attempts to rehabilitate the animal with their affection and care, the puppy's condition remains the same, and the couple is soon faced with the proposition of accepting a 12-year responsibility for which there is no foreseeable reward. The puppy offers no sense of companionship. It will never become a guard dog. It will not even give them the satisfaction of seeing it full of joy—for, ostensibly, it feels no joy. In the end, the couple does what most anyone else finding himself in such a situation would do. They put the dog into the back of their car and drive it to the animal shelter, trying to ignore as best they can what they know in their hearts to be

---

[1] The jīvātmā is the ātmā when ignorantly seen as conditioned by the body, mind and senses.

[2] Richard Ford, "Puppy," *The New Yorker*, December 24, 2001.

true: no one is ever going to pick it out as a pet and, after five days, it will be euthanized.

In the story, this is a difficult moment for the couple, but after they get home they quickly fall back into their hectic routines and, more or less, forget all about the dog. About a week later, the husband—who is narrating the story—suddenly remembers the dog, and realizes that, by now, it has most certainly been put to sleep. At this time he remorsefully reflects that the puppy was "a casualty of the limits we all place on our sympathy."

It is true. The compassion of one who has yet to understand his true self and fully assimilate that knowledge will always be limited. If we are honest, we will admit to seeing this in ourselves. Our compassion has borders, and when those borders are crossed, we retreat from kindness; we retract our generosity. We find ourselves saying things like, "I wish I could help, but I have to think of myself also." However, when reading this story it occurred to me that no one has ever fallen casualty to the limits of Amma's sympathy because Amma's sympathy and compassion simply have no limits.

The *ātma-jñānī*'s compassion has no limits because his sense of self has no limits. An individual's compassion ultimately ends where his sense of self ends. The *jñānī* understands that any perception of a boundary point wherein he ends and others begin is a misperception based on self-misconception and is to be ignored. As Amma said above when asked about her *darśan*, "The feeling of oneness is very real to me." This is why when Amma sees someone suffering, she immediately reaches out to comfort them. It is why, when she sees someone without a house, she wants to give them a house; why, when she sees someone without means to proper education, she wants to give them a proper education; why, when she sees someone without food, she wants to feed them; why, when she sees someone without love, she wants to love them. For Amma, the impulse to help others is as natural as the impulse to wipe the tears that fall from her own eyes.

Some time ago I heard a true story about a young doctor volunteering in a remote mountain hospital in Haiti.[1] It was past midnight, pouring rain, and she was desperately struggling to transport a seven-year-old boy dying from cancer to a more sophisticated institution. The tumor had started in his nasal region but had grown rapidly backward and was now pushing into his spine. The boy's life was fading, and the woman was literally racing against time, bouncing along the mountain roads in some poor excuse for an ambulance.

In fact, the hospital where she was trying to take the child was in America. The boy's only chance was through a procedure available only in Boston. Yet, all the while, in the young doctor's head a debate was raging: The boy was dying. Even if she got him to Boston, his chances were slim. He was going to have to be airlifted, and the cost was going to be more than $20,000. The head of her charitable institution was away, and she herself had pushed for the decision to move forward. Thus, as she bounced through the jungle to the airport, she doubted if she was doing the right thing. Was she wasting money that could be spent on other sick people with a higher chance of survival?

Eventually, the ambulance came to a bridge. Due to the massive rains, the stream over which the bridge passed was flooded and had risen beyond the height of the bridge-deck. Crossing would be extremely dangerous, but they had no choice. When the ambulance entered the bridge, the headlights submerged and everything went pitch black. Overcome with fear of her own mortality, the doctor found herself thinking, "I can't die. I have so much life left." Then, before she knew it, they were on other side—safe. She gave a sigh of relief, and instantly had a moment of clarity. She thought: "Okay, remember that: 'If it's your life, it's always the most important thing.'"

The young doctor realized that if it had been her lying there, there would be no question as to whether or not the $20,000 was an acceptable financial risk. She'd have risked the World Bank. Understanding this, she got the clarity to move forward without doubting her decision.

---

[1] Tracy Kidder, *Mountains Beyond Mountains: The Quest of Dr. Paul Farmer, A Man Who Would Cure the World*, Random House, 2003.

This is how it is with one who has become established in self-knowledge. Identifying with others' pain, fears, dreams and needs, the enlightened individual gives as readily as if they were his own.

There is one more important thing to note: While the *ātma-jñānī* willingly enters the chaos of the lives of the suffering, he himself never becomes lost in that chaos. If we observe Amma, at one level we can see the sorrow and joy of the people who come to her reflected in her. On another level, she never loses sight that her true nature is far-removed from anything and everything. I remember one time a journalist asked Amma what makes Amma happy, and Amma said, "On one level, the happiness of the world is Amma's happiness. When people are happy, Amma is happy. When people are sad, Amma is sad. However, in the innermost core, Amma is not attached to anything. She is always happy and peaceful in all circumstances, regardless of the external circumstances."

One Without a Sense of "Mine"

NIRMAMAḤ

Nirmamaḥ means that the *parābhakta* has no sense of "mine"—no sense of mine with regard to possessions, to achievements, to relationships, to anything external.

In the mid-1980s, Amma's *āśram* was just a few thatched huts. Even though we never felt it was austere because we were so immersed in Amma's love and compassion, the fact remains that we only had enough money to eat one full meal a day and sometimes we would even go without that. Myself and the other *brahmacārīs* only had a few decent shirts among us, and we would share them as per the need of the day. We never had a surplus of rice and vegetables. We lived completely hand-to-mouth. Since I had worked in a bank before joining the Āśram, I felt like I was the only one who really understood the importance of money. I was often irritated with how, despite our lack of resources, Amma was always giving funds donated to the Āśram to poor people. A woman would come telling Amma about her lack of money for her daughter's marriage, and the next thing I would know Amma would be calling someone to run and get the gold necklace that had been donated the day before. Knowing my place as a disciple, I would usually keep quiet, but inside I would be irritated, thinking, "Amma, we're poorer than she is!"

At one point, a man who was an expert in *vāstu śāstra*[1] visited the *āśram*. Seeing its layout, he immediately told me that it was inauspicious. He pointed to a large open area through which many people entered and exited. He said, "You cannot leave that space without a wall. If you do, all the Āśram's wealth will exit through there." I immediately brought him to inform Amma. Amma listened to him intently and then said, "Son, I want it like that. For worldly people, such a layout may be inauspicious because in their view life is

---

[1] Ancient Indian texts on the science of physical structures, with focus on architectural design, layout, measurements, ground preparation, space arrangement and spatial geometry.

about gaining money. Amma doesn't see things that way. This Āśram is not Amma's, nor is anything in it. It all belongs to the world. What is more auspicious than money leaving to help the poor and needy?"

Amma's view is that nothing is hers. The Āśram, its resources, its institutions, anything donated—everything belongs to the world, she says. Moreover, Amma always points out that even if we ostensibly possess something—be it an object, a relationship, an experience, etc—we will not be able to take it with us when we die. "Renounce ownership—consider all things as God's and enjoy them," she says. "This world is a temporary stop. You are here for a short period, as a visitor. Due to your ignorance, you divide everything, every inch of land, as yours and theirs. The piece of land you claim as your own has belonged to many others before. Now the previous owners are buried in it. Today, it may be your turn to play the role of owner, but remember, one day you too will disappear. Then another person will come and fill your shoes. So, is there any meaning in claiming ownership?"

Amma often says that the *jñānī* has no sense of "mine" because he does not see anything as separate from him. In order to see something as mine, I must first see that thing as existing outside of me: *my* house, *my* pen, *my* brother, *my* car... The *ātma-jñānī* has understood that not only is the *ātmā* his true essence, but it is also the essence of the entire universe—both the sentient and insentient. According to Vedānta, the *ātmā* is the ultimate subatomic particle, as it were. So, the *jñānī* knows that everything he sees within and without is nothing but he himself with a different superficial name and form. Seeing the world with this vision of oneness, how can he possibly call anything as "his"? It may be "him," but never "his." This is from the ultimate perspective, wherein all names and forms are understood to have one's own self as their substratum.

Here, some may have a doubt: "Other than the fact that a sense of ownership is an obstacle to *ātma-jñānam*, why would I want to attain it? The previous qualities—non-hatred, friendliness, compassion—all seem like nice things. However, some people derive a lot of happiness from owning things. We may doubt, "If I give up my sense of ownership, won't I actually lose out?" Amma says that it is just the opposite: "When we give everything, we are, in truth, gaining everything. When we surrender all the perishable things, what we realize in return is the imperishable *ātmā*—our true self. When we think, 'My land... *my* money... *my* children...,' etc, our world is contracting. When we renounce the attitude of 'mine,' everything becomes ours. Then, there are no differences. In that state, there is no difference between God and us. That is why it said that for one who knows the essence, the whole world becomes his wealth."

In fact, claims born of our sense of "mine" often render us foolish in the eyes of others. We become like the middleman for a hospital who, trying to get a commission for bringing in a patient, pushes his way to the front of a crowd standing around an accident victim. "Stand back! Clear the way! He's a relative of mine! He's a relative of mine!" he shouts. Yet, upon reaching the victim, the man sees not an injured human but a dead donkey—and everyone else sees not one jackass but two.

More importantly, it is, in fact, our sense of "mine" that is the source of all our worry in life. We don't worry about our neighbor's children; we worry about our children. We don't worry about our neighbor's health; we worry about our health. That said, just because we don't worry about our neighbor doesn't mean that we won't be there for him when he is in need. If he is sick, we may cook for him and help him clean the house, etc. If we see his child crying, we will hug the child, ask what is wrong and try to solve the problem. Despite helping our neighbor, we don't fret over his troubles. We lovingly do what is required and follow up if necessary, but we don't stay up all night worrying about whether or not the particular situation is going to be okay. So, in giving up the sense of "mine," the only thing we lose is anxiety.

Total eradication of our sense of ownership can only come from self-knowledge. This is because the foundation of our sense of ownership is our misunderstanding that we are limited by the body-mind-sense complex.[1] Self-knowledge directly destroys this misunderstanding and thus, indirectly, destroys the sense of ownership born of it.

How do we know if we are suffering from a sense of ownership? Very simple: worry. Worrying about something is a clear sign that we feel a sense of ownership toward it. When we find ourselves worrying over something, we should remind ourselves of these Vedāntic principles. When we worry about our children, we should remind ourselves that we neither own them nor, ultimately, can we even control them. We can only advise them and provide them support; we cannot force them to accept our advice. Many people think that worry is proof that we love someone, and if we don't worry about someone we don't really love them. This is total delusion. Worry has nothing to do with true love. It only has to do with a sense of possession. Moreover, worrying never helped anyone—neither the worrier, nor the one worried over. Analyze the situation, decide what you can and cannot do to help it, perform that action and then move forward.

Not feeling ownership with regards to our possessions and family members, etc, is not easy. This is one reason the *sannyāsī* does not own anything; his renunciation of all possessions and relations removes all scope for possession-based worry in his mind. This allows him the mental freedom to totally focus on self-knowledge until his understanding and resultant detachment are firm enough that, even if he were loaded with possessions, there could be no sense of ownership. However, Amma doesn't want us all to take *sannyāsa* and become monks. She says, what is most important is "inner *sannyāsa*." This is the inner conviction that none of our possessions or family members are really ours, but that, rather, they are all on loan from God, and God can take them back at any moment.

Amma often explains this inner-*sannyāsa* attitude with the example of the bird on the dry twig. She says, "A spiritually oriented householder should be like a bird perched on a dry twig. The bird knows that the twig can break at any moment. Therefore, it will be ready to take off at any time. Likewise, a householder should always

[1] Self-identification with the body-mind-sense complex is called ahaṅkāra. Its negation is the topic of the next chapter.

remain aware of the truth that his relationships and possessions will not always be with him. At any moment they can snap and he will have to fly."

So, if we want to reduce our sense of ownership, we should learn to start seeing everything that we previously consider as "ours" as "God's," remembering that God can take back the things he lent to us at any time.

In January 2001, when an earthquake with a magnitude of 7.6 hit the Bhuj District of Gujarat, a reported 20,000 people were killed, 167,000 were injured, 400,000 homes were destroyed and 600,000 people were rendered homeless. In March of 2002, Amma herself came to Bhuj in order to give *darśan* to the disaster victims and present them with the keys to 1,200 new homes the Āśram had built for them. When Amma asked them if they were sad about the loss of their loved ones, one of them responded, "Amma, we are not sad. God had given to us, and now He has taken away." This is inner *sannyāsa*—an attitude that must be there if we want to foster a mind that is free from worry, which is essential to attain *ātma-jñānam*.

One Without a Separate Sense of "I"

NIRAHAṄKĀRAḤ

The next sign of the *parābhakta*, Śrī Kṛṣṇa says, is *nirahaṅkāraḥ*. The word *ahaṅkāra* literally means "the 'I'-maker." Thus, *nirahaṅkāraḥ* means "one in whom the thought of 'I' has gone away."[1] Before we can understand what is meant by "eradicating *ahaṅkāra*," we first must understand what is meant by *ahaṅkāra*. We should note that the "I" itself is not the problem; the problem is our misconception regarding this "I." After all, the most famous Vedāntic statement from the Upaniṣads is *ahaṁ brahmāsmi*—"I am *brahman*."[2] Therefore, what the *ātma-jñānī* has eradicated is not his sense of "I," but his identification of that "I" with the body, mind and senses. That is, he has come to identify his "I" with pure awareness, pure consciousness. In that rediscovering of himself, he comes to clearly see that he is neither the one performing actions, nor the one undergoing the various experiences of life. Furthermore, he understands that he is not even the one willing his actions. He is, at best, a witness to all these phenomena. This is what is meant by *nirahaṅkāraḥ*.

The result of this knowledge is total freedom, total fearlessness, total selflessness. For just as self-knowledge frees us from the misconception of ownership when it comes to external objects [as explained in the previous chapter on *nirmamaḥ*], so too it frees us from this misconception with regard to the "internal" object of the body-mind-sense complex.

A famous story illustrates how a *jñānī* does not see himself as his physical body and the resultant detachment and selflessness that such an understanding can foster. Once a devotee was making a pilgrimage in the Himalayas. There he came across a wandering monk engaged in meditation. Seeing the radiant and peaceful look on the monk's face, the pilgrim reverently sat down at the his feet and waited for him

[1] From Śrī Śaṅkara's commentary: nirgatāhaṁ-pratyayaḥ—"one in whom the thought of 'I' has gone away."

[2] Bṛhadāraṇyaka Upaniṣad, 1.4.10

to open his eyes so that he could have his blessings. When he did so, he noticed that one of the monk's arms had a very bad infection. There were even maggots crawling on it. Soon the monk opened his eyes, saw the pilgrim sitting there and raised his hand to bless him. As he did so, one of the maggots fell off his arm and landed on the ground. The monk quickly reached down and picked up the maggot and placed it back on his arm, saying, "Oh, my little one. You almost lost your dinner."

The story is a bit extreme, but is what Amma does really so different? Ignoring the physically detrimental ramifications of embracing a million people every year, Amma—with total detachment—has offered her physical body to the world, allowing all of us to take spiritual and emotional nourishment from her physical embrace. Like the monk in the story, Amma doesn't see her body has hers; she sees it as the world's.

Nirahaṅkāraḥ does not end with disidentification from the body and senses. It also extends to disidentification with one's mind. Occasionally people directly ask Amma if she has attained self-realization. Amma always responds by saying that she makes no claims. Some people hear this and think Amma is just being humble. From one perspective, that is true, but the ultimate reason Amma makes no claims is that she doesn't identify with her mind. What is it that attains self-realization? The *ātmā* certainly does not attain it. The *ātmā* performs no actions and experiences no fruits. It is, at best, a mere witness and is ever liberated. What attains self-realization is the mind. Self-realization is the mental realization that one is the *ātmā*. Since self-realization is something that takes place in the mind, how can an *ātma-jñānī*—who identifies exclusively with the *ātmā*—ever respond "yes" to the question, "Are you self-realized?"

To better understand how the *jñānī*'s total identification with the *ātmā* leads to a sense of non-ownership from both external objects as well as from the body-mind-sense complex, it is helpful to compare the *ātmā* to light pervading a room. Many people may enter and exit the room, many events may take place there, but the light cannot claim ownership of, or identification with, any of these people and phenomena. So, too, it is with the self—the pure consciousness that pervades and illumines all of our thoughts, sense experiences and physical movements. Thus, the *ātma-jñānī* knows that, despite interacting with people at the level of the body, from the level of the *ātmā* there is no such interaction. He is the consciousness that illumines all experiences, but he himself has no experiences, no relationships, no possessions. Thus, there is nothing he can call "his."

There is a Malayalam *bhajan* Amma sings that presents this view of non-ownership with a beautiful metaphor:

> gandha-vāhanan pōle bandhiccu sarvattiluṁ
> bandhamillātte vazhān-uḷḷil nī vasikkaṇē[1]

The line above means: "O please dwell within me, helping me to live like the wind, having a bond with everything, yet being bound by nothing." Thus, the *ātma-jñānī*, knowing his true nature to be pure consciousness, knows that although the body interacts with various people and things and the mind has thoughts about various people and things, none of these ultimately have any connection with him, who is pure consciousness, pure awareness.

In meditation, we can clearly experience this. We can close our eyes, remain quiet and begin observing various phenomena that enter the stage of our mind: the perception of sound... the perception of a sensation... a feeling of impatience... a memory of Amma... a memory of our father... a desire to have coffee with a friend of ours... If we switch our focus from the phenomena to being the witness of the phenomena, we can see that none of these sense experiences, feelings, emotions, memories, ideas and desires—despite being mental phenomena—have any real connection with us, the witness.

Thus, "I" is not the problem. The problem is our erroneous understanding about "I." When we say, "I am the body," the "I" and the "am" are both very real. The only mistake is in our equating ourselves with the body-mind-sense complex. In truth, the correct

---

[1] "Cintakkaḷkk-Anytaṁ Vann-En Antaraṅgattil Ponturṁ"

statement is not "I am the body," but "I am pure bliss." The *ātma-jñānī* has realized this.

Another way of looking at this is that the *ātma-jñānī*'s sense of "I" has expanded to include the entire universe. On one level, he knows he is pure consciousness, but on another level he knows that this entire universe has manifested from that consciousness. Thus, his sense of self has become all-pervasive in that he knows that the ultimate building block of creation, as it were, is the consciousness that is he himself. Either way, he is *nirahaṅkāraḥ*—one without a limited sense of "I."

There is a beautiful Malayalam prayer that Amma sometimes quotes, which illustrates this second interpretation:

> ānanda-cinmaya harē gōpālikāramaṇa
> ñān-enne bhāvam-atu tōnnāyka vēṇam-iha
> tōnnunnatākilakhilaṁ ñān-itenna-vazhi
> tōnnēṇamē varada nārāyaṇāya namaḥ
>
> O Hari, who is pervaded with bliss and consciousness, in whom the gopikas delight, May I never feel the notion of "I." If I must, then let me feel "I am everything." O Giver of boons, I bow down to you, Nārāyaṇa.[1]

When discussing *nirmamaḥ* in the previous chapter, we said that the presence of our sense of "mine" is indicated by worry. Since the sense of "mine" is subtle, it is hard to view directly; we have to discover it by its symptom. *Ahaṅkāraḥ* is even subtler. Therefore, it is helpful to detect it via its symptoms as well. One of the primary symptoms of identifying with the body-mind is feeling that we are the doer—the agent of our actions. In fact, *ahaṅkāra* is often defined as this identification: "'I am the doer' is *ahaṅkāra*," says Tattva Bodha.[2] Anytime we get caught up in the feeling that "I am the doer," we can be assured that we are identifying with the body-mind. We can then use that as a reminder to bring back our Vedāntic understanding of our true nature.

---

1 Harināma-Kīrttanaṁ, verse 3, by Tuñcattu Rāmānujan Ezhuttacchan, 16th C.

2 Tattva Bodhaḥ, 7.3.2.2: ahaṁ-kartā ahaṅkāraḥ.

Obviously, it is not that the *ātma-jñānī* ceases to perform actions. On the contrary, he may perform more actions than one who is spiritually ignorant. However, irrespective of the *jñānī*'s level of activity, he can clearly demarcate himself from those actions. We will discuss this at more when we come to the quality of *śubhāśubha parityāgī* [one who renounces both the auspicious and inauspicious].

Other symptoms of *ahaṅkāra* are pride, arrogance, hubris, haughtiness, egomaniacal behavior, etc. In fact, these qualities are sometimes simply referred to as *ahaṅkāra*. This is because they are all rooted in the belief that this limited "I," comprised of the body and mind, is the ultimate reality. When we conceive of our self in this manner, the natural result will be two-fold: we will fear that we may be rendered even more limited, and we will long to become less limited.

Arrogance is a direct product of *ahaṅkāra* because the more identified one is with the limited self, the less willing he will be to acquiesce to the desires of others. Why? Because subconsciously he will feel that to do so is to concede a piece of himself, which he already perceives as being far too limited. Similarly, such a person will often try to impose his will upon others because he is trying to expand his sense of "I," to make it less limited, by controlling others. This is how arrogance and egomania, etc, arise from *ahaṅkāra*.

On the other hand, sometimes people appear to be humble, but their humility is merely an expression of an inferiority complex. An inferiority complex is just as much a symptom of *ahaṅkāra* as a superiority complex. In both cases, the individual has identified with his mind and the illusion it creates that "I am bound by the body-mind-sense complex." The only difference between the egomaniac and someone who suffers from an inferiority complex is that the former believes his "I" is superior to that of others, and the latter believes that his "I" is second-rate. In either case, their concepts are founded on ignorance about their true nature.

Since, *ahaṅkāra* and its eradication are inner phenomena, we cannot directly observe them in other people. However, in *mahātmās*, we can observe the humility born of non-identification with the body-mind. This is what we see in Amma—someone who is willing to bow down to anything and everything, someone who is always willing to listen to the input of others. Seeing the divinity within every aspect of creation—both sentient and insentient—the impulse to bow down before others is innate in Amma. As we said, Amma makes no claims with regard to her status; she has no feeling that "I am a great *ātma-jñānī*; let others bow down to me." Identifying not with the mind, but only with the *ātmā*, she is humbler than the humblest.

Every time Amma takes the dais, she bows down before everyone assembled. While I am used to this behavior of Amma's, there was one time that the profundity of Amma's humility struck me in particular. The occasion was a Sanskrit, English and yoga camp held at the *āśram* for children who had been affected by the 2004 Indian Ocean tsunami. On the final day of the camp, Amma came for a question-and-answer session with the children. In India, one bows down before another under one of several circumstances: the person should either be an elder, superior in a field of knowledge, a *sannyāsī* or a *mahātmā*. Yet, as soon as Amma stepped out before the children, she immediately offered her prostrations to all 6,000 of them. According to the traditional texts dealing with proper conduct[1], there was no reason for Amma to do this—she was older than all of them, certainly she was more knowledgeable, none of them were *sannyāsīs*, and Amma herself is a *mahātmā*. However, age is from the perspective of the body, and knowledge and spiritual greatness are from the perspective of the mind. Refusing to identify with either and seeing each child as an embodiment of the supreme, Amma spontaneously and sincerely offered her humble prostrations. In fact, I have not seen anyone else bow down before the audience like Amma. They may say, "I offer my prostrations to everyone," but who but Amma literally bows down?

---

[1] Dharma śāstras

One Who Is the Same in Hardship & Comfort

SAMA-DUḤKHA-SUKHAḤ

The next quality Śrī Kṛṣṇa gives for the *parābhakta* is *sama-duḥkha-sukhaḥ*—"one who is the same in sorrow and happiness." It is easy to become confused upon hearing this. It sounds like an oxymoron because it is referring to the mind of the *ātma-jñānī*, and a mind that is experiencing happiness is in no way the same as a mind that is experiencing sorrow. They are diametrically opposite experiences. Thus, we should be careful when we come across this expression, which appears often—not just in the Bhagavad-Gītā and other scriptures but also in talks by Amma. When we see this expression, we should take *duḥkha* and *sukha* not as the mental emotions of sorrow and happiness, but as circumstances in which it is common to experience sorrow and happiness. Examples of *duḥkha* would then be realizing your car has been stolen, learning you have failed an exam, hearing that someone you love has been diagnosed with an incurable disease, etc. Examples of *sukha* would be winning a million dollars in the lottery, learning you've been given a desired promotion, etc. If we take this interpretation, then Kṛṣṇa is saying that the *ātma-jñānī* remains mentally equipoised in both of these poles of experience. If someone tells him that they think he is great, he smiles serenely. If someone tells him they think he is an ignoramus, he also smiles serenely. Inside he remains blissful.

To understand why the *ātma-jñānī* retains mental equanimity despite whatever happens, it is helpful to look at why people who lack self-knowledge fail to do this. People become angry with someone when they think that person is obstructing the fulfillment of one of their desires. The more intense the desire, the more intense the anger. What dictates the intensity of the desire? Just as anger is directly proportional to desire, so too desire is directly proportional to how much one believes a particular object to be a source of happiness.

This is why an *ātma-jñānī* never becomes angry: He is not under the illusion that any object in the universe is a source of happiness. As such, his actions are never motivated by the desire to obtain happiness. Therefore, if someone prevents him from obtaining an object or doing an action, no anger results.

A question may arise: If an *ātma-jñānī* like Amma does not see any object in the universe, whatsoever, as a source of happiness, then where does his happiness come from? The answer is that it comes from the self, his true nature. The *jñānī* is, as Kṛṣṇa says in the Gītā, *ātmanyeva ātmanaḥ tuṣṭaḥ*—"Content in the self, through the self alone."[1] In fact, this is the very reason why he does not see any object as a source of happiness. He knows that there is only one source of happiness in the entire universe and that is the *ātmā*, which he has firmly understood and assimilated to be his true nature. When people develop a fondness for any sense object, be it a person, place or thing, it comes from the superimposition of the splendor that is in fact one's true nature onto that object.[2] The *ātma-jñānī* has no such error in perception.

As stated in the Introduction, all of these qualities enumerated by Kṛṣṇa are both effects of self-knowledge as well as required mental conditions for self-knowledge to take place. As such, true mental equanimity comes only as a result of *ātma-jñānam*. However, relative mental equanimity must be attained in order to understand and assimilate self-knowledge. The agitated mind is not really available for our use. Someone praises us and it is dancing on the ceiling; someone criticizes us and it is either depressed or fuming with anger. All of these various mental phenomena—depression, worry, anxiety, agitation, anger, excitement, over-elation—render the mind ineffective. A depressed mind can neither learn nor reflect nor ruminate on what it has learnt; likewise a mind soaring in elation. Such minds are unavailable in the here and now for serious spiritual pursuit. The primary spiritual practice for attaining this relative level of mental

---

[1] Bhagavad-Gītā, 2.55

[2] śobhana adhyāsaḥ

equanimity is *karma yoga*. Kṛṣṇa says this himself with his famous definition of *karma yoga*:

> yoga-sthaḥ kuru karmāṇi saṅgaṁ tyaktvā dhanañjaya |
> siddhyasiddhyoḥ samo bhūtvā samatvaṁ yoga ucyate ||
>
> Perform actions, O Dhanañjaya, being fixed in [*karma*] *yoga*—renouncing attachments and being mentally equanimous in success and failure. Equanimity is said to be [*karma*] *yoga*.[1]

However, we should understand that here, in the Amṛtāṣṭakam, Kṛṣṇa is not speaking about mental equanimity born of *karma yoga*. In *karma yoga*, we attain a relative amount of mental equanimity from accepting everything that comes to us in life—both hardships and fortunate circumstances—as God's *prasādam* [gift]. However, through that attitude, one will retain a sense of division between himself and God. He sees himself as God's devotee and performs his actions as a worship of God. Thus, a sense of non-identity with God is retained. *Ātma-jñānam* is the very knowledge that my true nature and God's true nature are one and the same: the eternally existent blissful consciousness that pervades all of creation. Thus, the *ātma-jñānī*'s mental equanimity comes not from seeing all things as God's gift but from his continued appreciation of the reality that bliss itself is his true nature and that all names and forms are but eternally changing superficialities to which he serves as the eternal substratum. As Sant Jñāneśvar writes in his commentary on this verse, "He is like the ocean, which is full even if it doesn't rain."

In his commentary on this quality, Śrī Śaṅkara makes an important point. He writes: "Whoever in whom hardship and comfort do not give rise to attachment or aversion is *sama-duḥkha-sukhaḥ*."[2] Śrī Śaṅkara is pointing out that when the *ātma-jñānī* undergoes a circumstance that most people would label adverse, it does not create within his psyche a negative impression that in the future will make him recoil from similar circumstances. Similarly, when he undergoes

---

[1] Gītā, 2.58

[2] duḥkhe-sukhe dveṣa-rāgeyoḥ apravartake yasya sa sama-duḥkha-sukhaḥ

a circumstance that most people would label pleasant or comfortable, no positive impression is made in his psyche that prompts him to pursue similar circumstances in the future. Only such a person can truly be considered free. Everyone else is simply reacting. It's not that the *ātma-jñānī* isn't aware of the law of cause and effect. Of course he knows that certain actions and circumstances will bring physical pain and problems and that certain others will bring physical comfort and ease. Nevertheless, his decisions are not dictated by that knowledge. It is but one minor factor for him to take into consideration when making his choices. The primary factor is the welfare of the world.

For example, as Amma does most every year, in July 2011, at the request of devotees, Amma travelled to Japan to give a week or so of programs there. The fact that parts of Japan were still considered dangerous due to spillage from nuclear reactors damaged by the Tōhuko Earthquake a few months before did not dissuade her. The other swāmīs and myself were not happy that Amma was going, but we at least took solace in the fact that the parts of Japan where Amma's programs were being held were far away from the danger zone. During the course of the programs, many victims of the disaster came for Amma's *darśan*. I could see the fear and insecurity fading from their faces as Amma compassionately showered them with her love and affection. Toward the end of the day, after Amma gave *darśan* to one more such victim of the disaster, Amma turned to the *brahmacārī* in charge of the Japan programs and said, "I'm going to go there." He didn't really take Amma seriously, but then a few minutes later Amma was asking him to start making the travel arrangements. The next day, Amma and the rest of us were in a caravan of cars driving to Tagajo, just 68 miles away from the still-leaking Fukushima Daiichi Nuclear Power Plant. Worse yet, in order to get there, we had to drive just 40 miles from the reactor itself. In Tagajo, Amma visited an evacuation center where more than 100 people who were still homeless were being accommodated. Despite the fact that no one could ensure us that the region was completely safe from the leakage, Amma stayed there, embracing, consoling, and wiping the tears of each and every person, showing us all what real courage and compassion are. Amma also visited the seashore in Shichigahama, offering prayers for the peace of those who had died and for the restoration of harmony between humankind and nature.

I mention this story because it perfectly illustrates how Amma, as a *sama-duḥkha-sukhaḥ*, is not guided by likes and dislikes but only by her selfless desire to console and care for suffering humanity. Did Amma know that going to the area was dangerous? Of course. Amma also knew that the trip itself would be difficult due to the post-disaster road conditions. Furthermore, she knew it would delay her arrival in Osaka, where she was scheduled to hold her next program, to the extent that she would arrive just a few hours before it was due to start. Yet, none of that deterred Amma. Due to her self-knowledge, her choices were not informed by selfish likes and dislikes but by her boundless love and compassion.

Another famous example is Amma's interaction with a leper named Dattan who was known for begging around Oachira, a town not far from the *āśram*. His wounds were so bad that Amma would only call him forward at the very end of *darśan*. Otherwise, seeing the blood and pus that Amma would get on her sāri from holding him, no one else would have followed for *darśan*. In the beginning, he was so putrid that, if I was standing beside Amma when he came for *darśan*, I would have to hold my nose. Yet, for years, Amma would not only hold him but she would tend to his wounds, cleaning his infected skin with her own lips and tongue. Seeing his physical recovery, it is my firm faith that Amma healed him. At the same time, I do not believe that this was the primary reason Amma would take him into her arms. I believe that whether Amma could heal him or not did not matter to her. Neither did whether or not she would become sick from their interactions. Her attitude was simple: "Let fate bring what it may, I will have dried the eyes of a child in pain." This is the type of freedom that comes from *ātma-jñānam*—the freedom to stop living in the shadow of our likes and dislikes and start living in the sunlight of a truly altruistic and expansive love.

Some people may ask, "What is wrong with being happy when good things happen and sad when bad things happen? Isn't that the nature of life?" There is nothing wrong with it, but we should understand that life doesn't have to be that way. If you want it to be that way, you are welcome to it, but if we reflect, we will see that when we allow objects to become sources of happiness for us, our joy and sorrow will be directly proportional. That is, as much joy as I experience when gaining a longed-for object, that much sorrow I will experience when losing it. Moreover, since every single thing in this universe is non-eternal, we will definitely one day lose every object we attain. Thus, as much joy we experience, that much sorrow. Viewing the human experience from this perspective, the scriptures refuse to term the enjoyment derived from sense objects as "happiness" at all. This is something Kṛṣṇa emphatically says in the fifth chapter of the Gītā:

> ye hi saṁsparśajā bhogā duḥkha-yonaya eva te |
> ādyantavantaḥ kaunteya na teṣu ramate budhaḥ ||
>
> Whatever enjoyments are born of contact [with sense objects] are verily wombs of sorrow alone; O Kaunteya, they have a beginning and an end. No wise man revels in these.[1]

If you enjoy such an arrangement, you are welcome to it. No one is forcing spirituality upon anyone. However, if you are aiming for the highest goal, then this attitude is insufficient. Moreover, we should also remember that, according to the scriptures, the pinnacle of happiness one can obtain through objects is but an infinitesimal fraction of the bliss that is our true nature: "Other beings live on a particle of this bliss alone."[2]

As discussed, before coming to Vedānta, we should try to cultivate equanimity, primarily through *karma yoga*: performing our professional work, our *seva*, any spiritual practices we do such as *japa* or meditation with the resolve that we are doing these actions only as a worship of God and have no wish for any material rewards from them. If grace in the material sphere comes, the *karma yogī* accepts it,

---

[1] Gītā, 5.22

[2] Bṛhadāraṇyaka Upaniṣad, 6.3.32: etasyaivānandasyānyāni bhūtāni mātrām-upajīvanti

but that is not his aim. His aim is simply to offer the worship to God and accept whatever comes to him in life—the so-called "good" and the so-called "bad"—equally, seeing them as God's gift. In this way, the *karma yogī* will become relatively equanimous and will experience some degree of contentment. This, in turn, will create a mind calm enough and steady enough to focus on Vedānta.

Once we fully understand Vedānta, we should shift the cause of our equanimity and contentment from seeing all things as God's *prasādam* to understanding that we ourselves are the source of all contentment, peace and bliss, and that all names and forms are but changing superficialities skating across the surface of our true self. Abiding in that bliss, let fortune come, let poverty come, let success come, let failure come—these things mean nothing to us now, for their relationship is only with the body and mind, and we know we are not the mind, but the witness consciousness—the *sākṣi caitanyam*—that illumines everything but is ever detached. As we move about in life, as we perform our work, do our *seva*, etc, we must reflect in this manner when the fruits of actions come our way. In closed-eye meditation, we should bring back the teaching that we are not the body, not the mind, but consciousness, detached, ever full and blissful. This cannot be just words. As we allow this thread of thought regarding our true nature to flow through our mind, we should affirm it as the truth of our inner reality and appreciate that the true "I" is, at best, a witness and not the performer of the actions, nor their instigator, nor the experiencer of their fruits.

One Endowed With Forgiveness

KṢAMĪ

Kṣamā literally means patience, the ability to forbear; a *kṣamī* is one endowed with that quality. *Kṣamā* can also be taken in the sense of "forgiveness" because forgiveness ultimately means having patience with other human beings, even when they have violated your sense of right and wrong. In such times, forgiveness is really our ability to accept their actions and not hold a grudge.

To understand the source of the *ātma-jñānī*'s forgiveness, we only need to review how willing we are to forgive ourselves because this is exactly how the *ātma-jñānī* sees other people—as his own self. If we are honest, we will see that we have infinite patience and forgiveness when it comes to our own transgressions. When we lose our temper with someone, we will say to ourselves, "Hey, it's okay. You were tired." When we fail to live up to our promises, we tell ourselves, "Hey, no one's perfect. Don't be so hard on yourself." We have a thousand ways to justify and then forgive our own actions. Seeing himself in all beings and all beings in himself, the *ātma-jñānī* is just as easy on other people as we are on ourselves. As Amma always says, "If we accidentally happen to poke our eye with our own finger, do we punish the finger? No. We simply try to soothe the pain. Why do we not punish the finger? Because both are part of us, both are ours. We see ourselves in both the eye and in the finger. In the same way, we should be able to see our own self in all beings. If we can do this, we can easily forgive the mistakes of others."

I would say that Amma can even be frustratingly forgiving. Sometimes when I am standing beside Amma people come to Amma to complain about someone else. Often, I think to myself, "He's got a good point. That person is very egoistic, and many people have complained about him to me before as well. In fact, I've even seen him in action myself." Like a fool, I start thinking that Amma is going to call and give that person a good dose. However, most of the time,

Amma will just say, "*Aw*... he is so *pāvam*.[1] He's very innocent. He works so hard." Everyone around Amma will probably be thinking, "He's not *pāvam*, Amma. He's a megalomaniac. In fact, he has other people do the majority of his work and takes all the credit." In such situations, even if, ostensibly, we are right, it is not that Amma is ignorant of the real situation. Trust me: Amma knows very well who is hardworking and who is lazy, who is humble and who is egoistic, who is sincere and who is feigning. At the same time, due to Amma's self-knowledge, her heart feels a unity with everyone and, just as we are very patient with ourselves, Amma has extreme patience with others as well. Although Amma wants all of us to cultivate good qualities and become more spiritually mature, she also knows that you cannot force a flower to bloom. You can only provide the proper conditions. Then you have to wait and let nature take its course. In Amma's own words, "We need to awaken from within. If Amma tries to force us to change, it's like trying to open an egg with a baby bird inside it from the outside. It will only end in destruction. When an egg breaks open from within, however, a new creation emerges."

Although Amma is the embodiment of patience, there are times when she realizes that continuing to externally accept a certain person's behavior will only feed that person's laziness or ego—times when she knows that what will be most beneficial is for her to speak up. So, while in general Amma doesn't like to push, if she knows that a good push is required, she will give it. Sometimes we need that. However, we should note that when Amma does chastise her disciples, this chastisement is also born out of that same feeling of oneness from which her patience and forgiveness come. I remember, speaking on this topic, Amma once commented, "I see the negativities of my children as my own negativities. Therefore, Amma will try to cultivate alertness and the ability to do the right thing in them. Just as a student is given tuition[2] for a subject in which he is weak, true help lies in helping others to correct their errors. Otherwise, what

[1] One deserving sympathy, Malayalam.

[2] Amma uses the English word "tuition" in its sense of private tutoring sessions.

is the meaning in them calling me 'Amma' [mother] and me calling them 'children'?"

Amma's display of patience with her disciples and devotees may terminate at a point when she feels that they require her intervention to move forword. However, when it comes to people who are not disciples or devotees, Amma's patience seems limitless. There have been occasions when such people have even told blatant lies about Amma and the Āśram in order to try to tarnish Amma's name. Regardless, Amma sees such people as infants—people who have yet to attain a level of maturity wherein they are capable of learning from correction. As such, Amma's response has always been one of forgiveness. I remember on one of these occasions, a newspaper reporter asking Amma if she was planning any reprisal. Amma responded by asking the reporter a counter question: "If the baby kicks the mother, does the mother kick the baby in return?"

This is how an enlightened soul views the transgressions of humankind—both those in general and those specifically against him. He sees them simply as the actions of ignorant people—infants. The *ātma-jñānī* will never hit back when hit or insult back when insulted. He will never harbor any thoughts of spite or revenge. He will never malign the character of the person attacking him. Not only that, he may not even stop helping such people. He simply accepts their actions, never having expected them to act any differently in the first place.

There is a famous story Amma sometimes tells that demonstrates this quality of the enlightened soul. A *mahātmā* saw a scorpion drowning by the bank of a river. He immediately reached down and scooped it out to save it. Immediately, he was stung and dropped it. Again he picked it up, and again he was stung. Yet, he picked it up a third time. At this point, a passerby asked the *mahātmā* why he was helping the creature despite its actions. The *mahātmā* replied, "It is the scorpion's nature to sting; it is my nature to help."

In the story, the *mahātmā* has no expectations regarding the scorpion. Amma says, in fact, it is from our unrealistic expectations with regard to the behavior of other people that a lot of our anger and desire for revenge come. She says that we should drop these expectations. In her own words, "See a frog as a frog and an elephant as an elephant. Don't try to make the cat into a dog or a dog into a cat." The *mahātmā* knows that very few people have self-knowledge and even fewer have assimilated that knowledge fully. Thus, most simply act according to their tendencies. Some have cultivated good tendencies and thus are capable of acting in a responsible manner. Some are trying to do this but have yet to accomplish it. Others are still completely in the grip of their selfish desires. Understanding that this is the nature of the world, the *mahātmā* accepts everything as God's play. Sometimes, God's play is a comedy, sometimes a tragedy. Regardless, the *mahātmā*, like a dispassionate audience member, simply witnesses, never giving the play any more reality than it deserves.

When explaining this quality, Śrī Śaṅkara says that even when the *ātma-jñānī* is physically or verbally abused, he remains unperturbed.[1] This implies a mind in which reaction to insult and violence does not enter even as an impulse to be swiftly rejected. Such complete patience and forgiveness are only possible as effects of fully assimilating *ātma-jñānam*. They are born of the *ātma-jñānī*'s total disidentification with his physical body and total identification with the *ātmā*. When someone is abusing the *ātma-jñānī*, regardless of how he chooses to respond physically or verbally, within he always remains unaffected. It's like that old joke wherein a police officer sees a man leaning against an illegally parked car and issues him a ticket. The man responds, "If you think I'm moving this car just because you've written that ticket, you're a fool." The policeman then smashes the car's headlight and writes another ticket for the newly observed violation. The man says, "I said, 'You'd be a fool,' because it's not my car." This is how it is when someone tries to get a rise out of the *ātma-jñānī* by insulting him. To him, it's like the insulter is speaking about someone else.

We may feel that, in some cases, forgiving someone and not feeling hatred at the thought of them, is too much—that only an *ātma-jñānī* is capable of such a thing. However, remember, our mind requires at

---

[1] ākruṣṭaḥ abhihito vā avikriya eva āste.

least a relative amount of all of these qualities in order even to be fit for self-knowledge. As is said in Kaṭha Upaniṣad:

> nāvirato duścaritānnāśānto nāsamāhitaḥ |
> nāśānta-mānaso vā'pi prajñānenainam-āpnuyāt ||
>
> One who has not desisted from bad conduct, whose senses are uncontrolled, whose mind lacks concentration, whose mind is unpeaceful, cannot attain this [the self] through knowledge.[1]

The fact is, even without self-knowledge, we are capable of tremendous amounts of patience and forgiveness. If we have mentally tuned with Amma and her teachings, we can invoke these higher aspects of ourselves. In reality, the person who has insulted or abused us loses nothing by our bitter feelings. On the other hand, since hatred and revenge are by nature agitating thought patterns, we ourselves lose out on peace of mind. By holding on to such feelings, we are only harming ourselves, or from another angle, we are allowing that person to continue to harm us. Amma says this phenomenon is common amongst divorcees. She says that many people who have undergone divorce tell her that, due to the betrayal and mean-spirited behavior they suffered at the hands of their former spouse, they refuse to forgive. Many have told Amma, "I can forgive anyone, but don't ask me to forgive him." In such cases, Amma points out how, even after the divorce, the individual's mind is still ruled by the former spouse. "Although we have been released from one perceived jail, we remain behind the jail bars of our own mental creation," Amma says. "Forgiveness is the medicine that heals the wounds of the heart. By forgiving others, we are not doing them a favor; we are helping ourselves." Viewed from this perspective, letting go of bitter experiences and forgiving is clearly in our own best interest. Furthermore, as the Kaṭha Upaniṣad mantra points out, if we want to have a mind capable of the degree of inner observation and discernment required for truly appreciating, assimilating and remaining steadfast in spiritual knowledge, then we absolutely must let such things go.

[1] Kaṭha Upaniṣad, 1.2.24

The following incident, which was shared with me by the *brahmacārī* involved, illustrates the extent to which forgiveness is possible—even for one who has yet to understand his oneness with all of creation. It took place in the mid-1990s. Back then, every Saturday in Amritapuri was a day of fasting. Except for those whose health problems precluded it, all of the *āśram* residents would fast on Saturdays until around 9:00 p.m., when Amma would come to the roof of the temple and serve everyone pudding as *prasādam*. One such evening, this *brahmacārī*, who was relatively new at the time, was sitting at Amma's side. As he explained to me later, he was not very used to fasting and was extremely hungry. He had already received his share of pudding, but in the *āśram* one doesn't just eat upon receiving his food. He will wait for everyone else to receive their share, then wait for the unison chanting of the 15th chapter of the Bhagavad-Gītā, then wait for Amma to have a bite. Only then will one eat. While all this was going on, this *brahmacārī* was secretly praying for only one thing: "Let them serve fast and chant fast!" Finally, all the serving and chanting was complete, but instead of taking a bite Amma turned to this *brahmacārī* and said, "I think the orphans from Parippalli[1] just arrived. Bring them here." A little irritated, this *brahmacārī* went downstairs, found the 100 or so orphans who had just arrived and brought them back up to the roof of the temple. Of course, Amma wanted to distribute pudding to all of them as well. However, it turned out that there wasn't enough. So, Amma asked all the *brahmacārīs* and *brahmacāriṇīs* to give back one scoop of their pudding. This *brahmacārī* couldn't believe it. Worse yet, when the person came to him to take the pudding from his plate, he took two scoops, not one. Seeing this, he thought to himself: "Amma, this isn't fair. I'm sure these children had a nice breakfast, a nice lunch and a nice dinner just an hour or so ago. I've been fasting and doing *seva* all day." Just as he was thinking like this, a little girl came up to Amma for her share, and Amma gave her not one but two scoops. The *brahmacārī* told me that, at this point, he was almost angry with

[1] Amma's orphanage, located in Kollam District, Kerala

Amma. At that very moment, Amma turned to him and said, "Just because you're sitting next to me, don't think you are close to me." Amma pointed to one of the little girl's eyes. It was milked over and obviously blind. Amma said, "Do you know how that happened? Before we took her into the orphanage, her father came home drunk one night and put his cigarette out in her eye." Tears formed in Amma's eyes, but she quickly wiped them away with the edge of her hand. She continued, "When she first came for *darśan*, Amma asked her what had happened. Do you know what she said after telling me? She said, 'Amma, please promise me you will not punish my father. He was drunk at the time and didn't know what he was doing.'" Amma looked hard at the *brahmacārī* and repeated, "So, don't think you are close to me just because you are sitting by my side."

This story illustrates two important principles. First, it provides us with a good example of Amma giving a disciple some "tuition." Seeing the *brahmacārī*'s lack of compassion for the orphans as a drawback of her own and knowing that the time was ripe to draw his attention to it, Amma did so. Her words may have been cutting and serious, but this was only a tool to help drive home her point. Inside, Amma definitely remained peaceful. As Amma says, "The anger of a *mahātmā* is like a burnt rope. It looks just like a real rope, but if you touch it, you will see that nothing is really there." In fact, since the *brahmacārī* took Amma's scolding with the right attitude, it was a moment of tremendous grace for him, helping to draw him out of the petty world of his own personal concerns and into a more expansive world of compassion. Secondly, the incident illustrates the level of forgiveness we should be striving to cultivate. Moreover, remember, this is not the forgiveness of an *ātma-jñānī*, but simply that of a child who had somehow imbibed the value as a part of her regular outlook on life.

If we have truly understood the teachings regarding our true self, we should strive to assimilate this quality as a natural extension of that understanding. This means, each time we are insulted and feel a negative reaction arising, we should reflect on who we truly are in a spiritual sense and dissolve the power of that arising thought through discernment. If we can reflect in this manner when such situations arise, not only can we nip such ignorance-steeped thoughts in the bud, we can also gradually reduce our tendency to react in the first place. This process takes time and dedicated effort, but gradually it has its effect.

Here, a doubt may arise: Since forgiveness in its full glory can only be a product of *ātma-jñānam*, how can we develop this value to the extent required to attain that self-knowledge? There are a number of methods for cultivating forgiveness. One, we have discussed: Not having expectations. Amma says that we should realize that all worldly love has some degree of selfishness in it. When we understand this, we will stop expecting others to behave like saints and we will be much more accepting and patient when they commit selfish, egocentric actions. Another method is to have faith in the law of karma, which states that every single experience we undergo—be it at the hands of Nature or at the hands of other people—is, in fact, the fruit of an action that we have performed either earlier in this life or in a past life. When we can reflect, upon being insulted, that the insult was the karmic fruit of, perhaps, our having insulted someone else in the past, it is easier to let go of feelings of hatred and revenge because to take revenge would only perpetuate the cycle. We can also simply look at the lives of other saints and sages and see how they were able to forgive. This will inspire us to do so as well. In these and other ways, we can go a long way toward cultivating patience and forgiveness.

In the case of the little girl forgiving her father, it's impossible to say the exact source of her capacity for forgiveness. Regardless of how she attained the capacity to forgive him, the important thing is to see that forgiveness is possible and that we have to put in effort to cultivate it if we want to imbibe true spirituality.

Before concluding, I would like to make one more important point. Just because Śrī Śaṅkara says that the *ātma-jñānī* is unperturbed even when hit or insulted doesn't mean that we should not stand up for ourselves and for others. If people are physically harming us, we should react—if only just to run away. What is important is that mentally we are unaffected. Even if we have to battle it out externally, within we should remain peaceful and devoid of hate. For non-*sannyāsīs* who are transacting in the world, it is incorrect to allow others to walk all over you. As Amma always says, "If someone comes in the room with a machinegun, we cannot just sit there, saying, 'Non-violence is the ultimate dharma.' We must react. If we fail to react, instead of just one or two people being injured, dozens may be injured. Then our non-reaction itself has in fact become a form of violence." Furthermore, until we have cultivated the spiritual maturity to accept the aggression of others toward us as Amma has, we should continue to respond, making sure we do so through righteous means.

In general in spiritual life, we need to know and accept our own level. Otherwise, we can end up like the egg that imitated the orange. ("One day before breakfast, an orange rolled off the counter and escaped its fate. Filled with hope, the egg followed.") I remember a few years ago, Amma was talking with someone who was undergoing a lot of personal problems, including that various people he cared about were spreading lies about him and trying to bring lawsuits against him. As part of her advice to him, Amma explained that, during certain astrological periods in an individual's life, no matter what the affected person does, it will be taken in the wrong way. She said that during such periods one should try to perform good deeds. Even though these also may be taken in the wrong way, they will lessen the affects of the previous bad actions. The man nodded and said, "I understand. I should start doing more loving acts in the world." Amma softly said, "Yes." Then the man said, "So, the best defense is no defense." To which Amma said, "No. I can follow that path because I can accept anything that comes, but you are not at that level. So, you must also stand up for yourself and deal with the situation."

One Who Is Ever Content

SATATAṀ SAṀTUṢṬAḤ

The next quality mentioned by Śrī Kṛṣṇa is *satataṁ saṁtuṣṭaḥ*. *Satataṁ* means always; *saṁtuṣṭaḥ* means one who is perfectly content, perfectly satisfied, one who has no feeling of lacking or wanting, one who feels ever complete. Kṛṣṇa has already explained the cause of the *parābhakta*'s contentment in the Gītā's second chapter as coming directly from his own self: "Content in the self by the self alone."[1]

For most of us, the idea of being permanently self-content is hard to even conceive because our personal experiences of contentment have always come in the wake of the fulfillment of various desires: obtaining a job, eating a delicious meal, winning the love of our dream partner, having our adult children spend the holidays with us, etc. However, the contentment of an *ātma-jñānī* is not based on the attainment of such things; it is founded in the self.

According to Vedānta, a desire is nothing but a repetitive thought wave—be it gross and acute or subtle and obtuse—fixating our mind upon a certain attainment. These desires are based upon past impressions formed in our psyche associated with similar situations. For example, we feel lonely. The last time we felt lonely, we called our friend and we felt better. Thus, now, the very feeling of loneliness triggers the desire to call our friend, and we decide to act upon it. However, when we call him, his number is busy. The pressure of the thought waves pushing us to fulfill the desire builds. We try again; again the number is busy. "Who is he talking to? When is he going to get off the phone? I need to speak to him now!" The desire intensifies. The mind becomes even more turbulent with that desire. We try again, and he finally answers. The desire is filled, and the turbulence in the mind is quelled instantly. That is, the desire thought waves clouding the mirror of the mind are eradicated, and we experience the contentment that is, in reality, a mental reflection

---

[1] Bhagavad-Gītā, 2.55: ātmanyevātmanatuṣṭaḥ

of our own true nature. This is how contentment based on fulfilling one's desires works.

Unfortunately, such contentment can never be "constant." It lasts only until the next desire arises. For most of us, this is only a matter of a few minutes. Furthermore, we have only deepened the furrow in our psyche that associates calling a friend with the relief of loneliness. The deeper the furrow, the more intense the desire. The more intense the desire, the greater the mental turbulence. The greater the mental turbulence, the more disturbed our peace. Worse yet, our friend is not always going to be there to pick up the phone. Therefore, if our peace and contentment depend on that condition, eventually we are going to suffer.

The *ātma-jñānī* knows that bliss is the nature of the self. He understands that any happiness anyone seems to experience through objects, relationships, situations, etc, is only that individual's true nature shining forth. He also knows that desire itself creates the mental conditions that obstruct one's true nature from reflecting in the mind. With this knowledge, he refuses to play the mind's game. This allows him to bathe in the source of bliss—himself—rather than going through the troublesome, unreliable middleman of desire-fulfillment.

In Vedānta, we often hear the expression *saccidānanda ātmā*: the self that is *sat*, *cit* and *ānanda*—existence, consciousness, bliss. With a little study and reflection, we can soon understand that we are always existent and conscious. However, the bliss aspect creates confusion because, although sometimes we feel blissful, we do not always feel that way. Here, it is helpful to understand that every instance of happiness, or bliss, that we experience—be it in deep sleep, in meditation or in day-to-day life—is the result of the creation of a mental condition that is congruous with the expression of our true self. Conversely, every experience of sorrow, frustration, anger, etc, is the result of the creation of a mental condition incongruous with the expression of our true self. However, regardless of our temporary mental conditions, the substratum of *saccidānanda* remains constant. We can explain this phenomenon with the example of various atmospheric conditions. On a sunny day, the sun is clearly experienced. On a cloudy day, although the sun is still there, it will barely be felt. The mind is akin to the atmosphere. Certain conditions allow the bliss of the self to shine within it; certain conditions do not. Regardless, the bliss remains, and the reflection points to the existence of the original.

Perfect constant contentment is only possible through understanding our true nature because only the *ātmā* is eternal. If our contentment is based on any other entity in the universe—be it a person, place, thing, attainment, relationship, etc—its foundation will be unsound. Then it is not a question of if our contentment will go, only a question of when. If it came as an event in time, it will go as an event in time. While perfect contentment only comes through self-knowledge, we can attain a relative amount of contentment through *karma yoga*[1] and through reflecting on the transient nature of all things other than the *ātmā*. The majority of people have yet to understand that only the *ātmā* is eternal. However, as spiritual seekers, we must begin to internalize this understanding. Until we do so, our mind will always be turning outward in hopes of finding contentment in the objects of the external world. Someone once showed me a scene from a film called *Dumb & Dumber* (1994) that illustrates this truth. Throughout the comedy, the protagonist has been desperately pursuing a woman who is not interested in him. Unable to read her obvious signals, he begs her to level with him and tell him his chances of winning her heart. She tells him, "Not good." He responds, "You mean, not good like 'one out of a hundred'?" She responds, "I'd say, more like one out of a million." The man celebrates, saying, "So, you're telling me there's a *chance*!" Until we are convinced that true contentment is only possible in and through the self, we will continue to search for it in the material world.

And let's say that somehow we were able to conjure a desired object that was miraculously eternal. What would happen? Of course, we would eventually grow tired of it. Isn't that our experience? Everything in this world leaves us wanting. So many of the things we've wanted in life, we've already attained: jobs, relationships, possessions, homes,

---

[1] For an explanation of karma yoga, refer to the chapter on sama sukha-duḥkhaḥ.

children, grandchildren, success... But are we content? For most of us, there is still that feeling of lacking. Vedānta boldly tells us that the things of this world will never take away that feeling.

As said, if we want to attain contentment, we have to spend time reflecting on these truths—that nothing we have is eternal and that nothing we attain will give us perfect contentment. Each time, a desire rises in our mind, we should reflect like this, bringing these truths back to our mind. We need not become a *sannyāsī*, with no possessions or professional ambitions, but when we obtain something or strive to obtain something, we should be very clear regarding that thing's impermanent nature and its inability to make us eternally content. As a Sanskrit saying goes:

> arthānām arjane duḥkham arjitānāṁ ca rakṣaṇe |
> āye duḥkhaṁ vyaye duḥkhaṁ dhig-arthāḥ kaṣṭa-saṁśrayāḥ ||

> Acquisition of wealth is painful, so too the effort to protect wealth.
> Pain in gain, pain in loss—Alas! Wealth is home to hardship.

The practice of reminding ourselves of these truths cultivates *vairāgyam*—detachment from the objects of the world. Without detachment, our mind will never really be available to us for serious spiritual pursuit. It will constantly be nagging us to obtain some object or the other. It won't let us spend time focused on our spiritual studies or practices. In fact, the opposite of contentment is greed, and an individual who has fallen prey to greed can never hope to realize the self. Why? Because greed itself—irrespective of its focus—has as its cause the misconception that contentment can be attained through amassing more. Greed believes happiness is attainable through the material.

The detached mind quickly rejects such erroneous thoughts. If worldly desires arise in such a mind, they are nipped in the bud by its discrimination. Thus, the detached mind shuts down the desires and thought patterns that are inconducive to the spiritual goal or incongruous with self-knowledge, thus helping us to live a spiritual life.

In fact, even after we have understood the spiritual teachings regarding the *ātmā*, this practice of reminding ourselves of the impermanence of any happiness that is not founded directly on the *ātmā* has to continue. For Vedāntic meditation is based on two truths: *brahma satyam* and *jaganmithyā*. Literally, this means "*brahman* is real" and "the universe is an illusion."[1] However, we should expand the meaning to bear out an important point: "The happiness that comes directly from *brahman* [*ātmā*] alone is real and permanent; the happiness that comes from the objects of the world is temporary." Thus, in Vedāntic meditation, we can meditate on either side of this coin. We can meditate on the self, affirming it as the true eternal blissful reality of who we are. Or we can meditate on the world, reminding ourselves that the happiness we seem to derive from its objects is temporary and really not coming from the objects at all but from within us.

For us, it may be difficult to conceive of being *satataṁ saṁtuṣṭaḥ*—ever perfectly content—but for someone like Amma who has assimilated the Vedāntic wisdom, it is the constant experience. Amma's contentment requires nothing external whatsoever.

[1] Although mithyā literally means "illusion," Vedānta explains this does not mean unreal in the sense of something that does not exist. Rather it means unreal in the sense that its reality is temporary and depends completely upon its non-temporary substratum, like rope that appears to be a snake or a post that appears to be a ghost.

One Whose Mind Is Concentrated

YOGĪ

A lot of confusion surrounds the term *yogī*. The main reason for this confusion is that the word has different meanings depending on its context. It comes from the Sanskrit root *yuj*, which has a number of meanings, including to join, to unite. Thus, in the scriptures, the term *yogī* can refer to a person "joined" in any spiritual practice—*karma yoga*, meditation, *jñāna yoga*, etc. It can also mean a self-realized individual who has "joined" his *jīvātmā* [individual soul] with the *paramātmā* [supreme soul] through the knowledge that they were always one and the same. However, the primary meaning of *yuj* is to concentrate the mind, and that is how Śrī Śaṅkara takes it here, defining a *yogī* as a person with a concentrated mind—*samāhita-cittaḥ*.

The *ātma-jñānī*'s powers of concentration and mental control are unparalleled. When Amma decides to focus on something, nothing can deter her. I remember once, during the meditation part of a program of Amma's in Tokyo, everything suddenly began to vibrate with the tremors of an earthquake. Everyone, myself included, opened their eyes and looked around—only to see Amma sitting with eyes still peacefully closed, rapt in meditation. If Amma makes a resolve to meditate for a specific period of time, nothing can disturb her. In the same vein, when Amma is dealing with a serious issue—for example, relief work in the wake of a natural disaster—she also has the concentration to see that work through until the end without getting sidetracked. Her mental control is flawless.

I am reminded of the old days, when myself and the other now-*sannyāsī* disciples of Amma were first coming to see her. As I've mentioned, back then we did not know much about spirituality. We were primarily interested in experiencing Amma's motherly compassion. We enjoyed talking with her and joking with her, but of course Amma had other plans—specifically to prod us forward along the spiritual path. So, after conversing with us for a while Amma would usually sit in meditation in hopes that by seeing her example we would spend some time refining our minds through this discipline. The problem was that Amma's capacity for meditative concentration and our capacity were light years apart. After 20 or 30 minutes, our eyes would open and we would want to resume the talking and joking. To our chagrin, Amma would not open her eyes when we would. Like a good athletic coach who is always pushing his trainees to run further or jump higher, Amma wanted us to try to meditate for longer and longer, to strengthen our power of concentration and mental control. The only way she could push us was to refuse to open her eyes.

The ability to focus is essential for a successful pursuit of Vedānta. In order to study the scriptures and words of the guru, we must be able to sit with focus and concentration. Our mind cannot drift this way and that. We cannot be like the disciple Amma sometimes jokes about who, instead of listening to his guru, began watching a mouse crawl around a hole in the wall. Then, when the guru asked him if the teaching had "gone in" yet, he replied, "Not completely. Its tail is still out." Thus, concentration is required for the fundamental Vedāntic spiritual practice of *śravaṇam*—listening to the Vedāntic teachings. Just as it is required for listening, it is also required for *mananam*—reflecting upon the teachings and identifying and clearing our doubts. Furthermore, once our Vedāntic understanding is doubt-free, concentration is also required for *nididhyāsanam*—the practice of dwelling in that knowledge and systematically removing the habitual actions, words and thoughts that run contrary to it.

It is through this third practice that our self-knowledge becomes firm. Śrī Kṛṣṇa calls this the conversion of mere *prajñā* [knowledge] into *sthitaprajñaḥ*—fixed, steadfast, firmly entrenched and assimilated knowledge.[1] Only when our knowledge becomes steady can we truly be said to be an *ātma-jñānī* in the ultimate sense of the term. Moreover, only when our knowledge is firmly established via *nididhyāsanam* will we gain the degree of concentrative power that we observe in someone like Amma. This is because Amma's power of concentration is not only born through spiritual practices like meditation; it is also

[1] Gītā, 2.61

born from her heartfelt understanding that the self is the sole source of fulfillment and that everything other than pure consciousness is ephemeral. Ultimately this understanding is what will make our power of concentration complete because when we grasp "I am bliss," etc, as a living truth, it strips the various enticing objects of the world of their power to draw our attention without our permission. Thus Vedāntic assimilation and concentration go hand in hand—each one fuels the other until we find that mental discipline is no longer a discipline but our natural, spontaneous mode of functioning. Ultimately, here in the Amṛtāṣṭakam, Kṛṣṇa is speaking about an *ātma-jñānī*. Therefore, when he says *yogī*, he not only means that this individual has concentration of mind in a general sense, but that he never loses awareness of the Vedāntic truth he has learned regarding his true nature and the true nature of the world in which he transacts.

Meditation, chanting one's mantra, chanting *stotrams* like the Lalitā Sahasranāma, etc, are all means to cultivate our power of concentration. If the practice involves focus, the mind's capacity to focus will increase. As Amma says, "Whatever form of meditation we do, whether we focus on the heart or between the eyebrows, the goal is the same—one-pointed concentration." Thus, such spiritual practices can and should be practiced from the very outset of spiritual life. Just as a daily regimen of lifting weights strengthens the physical body, so too a daily regimen of focused meditation strengthens the mind. The less subtle the object of our meditation, the less difficult it will be to focus on that object. Thus, singing *bhajans* with concentration, chanting mantras, meditating on God with form, etc, are all prescribed. Once we have understood Vedānta fully, our meditation is no longer upon any object, regardless of how subtle the form may be, but upon ourselves—meditation upon the meditator. This is not easy. It cannot be done in the beginning. In order to engage in Vedāntic meditation, one must first have studied and attained a doubt-free understanding of Vedānta and also gained the mental strength required to focus on such a subtle principle. Thus non-Vedāntic forms such as those mentioned above are an essential foundation.

One Who Is Self-controlled

YATĀTMĀ

The next quality is *yatātmā*—one who has controlled his own nature.[1] Before coming to Vedānta, as well as during its study and assimilation, the *ātma-jñānī* put in intense effort to discipline his mind. When unhealthy thoughts and negative thinking would arise, he would quickly discern that these thoughts were harmful and terminate them. Similar was his discipline regarding sense objects. He would avoid people, objects and situations that were counterproductive to his spiritual goal—objects that, for example, seemed to reinforce the misconception that happiness is rooted in the experience of external phenomena. Thus, through steadfastness in these two disciplines—known in the scriptures as *śamaḥ* and *damaḥ* [mental and sense control], respectively—by the time one has attained self-knowledge, mental and sensory discipline have become a spontaneous, natural part of his personality. Moreover, his disciplined nature is then bolstered by his Vedāntic understanding. Seeing the essential oneness of himself, God and the universe, he is no longer prone to the negative thinking and sense-oriented desires that arise from the perception of duality. Thus, through his knowledge and his disciplined nature, he has become ever in control of his thoughts, words and actions.

The more one assimilates *ātma-jñānam*, the more spontaneous and natural self-control becomes. At the same time, the more mentally and sensually disciplined one becomes, the easier it becomes to assimilate self-knowledge. Therefore, mental and sensory discipline are essential for all spiritual seekers. *Śama* is founded on the principle that although we do not have control over the thoughts that pop into our head, we do have control over whether we entertain those thoughts or not. If we want a mind that is psychologically healthy enough to gain and retain true understanding of our real nature, this thorough weeding out of potentially harmful thoughts is essential. All harmful

---

[1] Śrī Śaṅkara's gloss: saṁyata-svabhāvaḥ

and negative thinking should be nipped in the bud. Through such effort, we can gradually transform our thinking patterns.

Sometimes when discussing the phenomenon of how such discipline can transform our nature, Amma will give the example of Tumban, a street dog that sometimes sleeps in her room. When he first began staying there, Amma would promptly send him out as soon as the 4:00 a.m. bell rang for the morning *arcana*. After a month or so, Amma says she no longer had to send him out at this time. A few minutes before the bell would strike, he would be waiting at the door, ready to scamper down the steps into the prayer hall. Actions beccome habit, and habits become our nature.

Thought regulation is a vital spiritual practice. It is not only requisite prior to coming to Vedānta, but it also must be maintained during the process of studying and assimilating Vedānta. In fact, in the second chapter of the Gītā, Kṛṣṇa stresses the importance of maintaining mental and sensory discipline, saying that they are essential auxiliary practices even for one who has intellectually understood Vedānta and is now doing Vedāntic meditation as his primary spiritual practice. Thus Kṛṣṇa makes it very clear that performing quality control with regard to our thoughts, etc, is not only for spiritual beginners. On the contrary, Kṛṣṇa is prescribing this discipline even for advanced Vedāntic students. Kṛṣṇa strongly stresses that if one fails to adhere to thought discipline in particular, a spiritual fall is bound to occur:

> dhyāyato viṣayān-puṁsaḥ saṅgasteṣūpajāyate |
> saṅgāt sañjāyate kāmaḥ kāmāt-krodho'bhijāyate ||
> krodhād-bhavati saṁmohaḥ saṁmohāt-smṛti-vibhramaḥ |
> smṛti-bhraṁśād-buddhi-nāśo buddhi-nāśāt-praṇaśyati ||

> For the man who mentally dwells on objects, fondness for them arises. From fondness, desire [to attain them] is born. From [thwarted] desire, anger is born. From anger, comes delusion [with regard to what is dharma and what is adharma]; from that delusion comes the [temporary] inability to remember [the spiritual teachings one has learned]; [with repeated occurrences] from that [temporary] inability to remember comes the [permanent]

> destruction of that capacity. From that destruction, one's [spiritual] life is destroyed.[1]

Here we see how important mental discipline is. Once we truly attain the goal, like Amma, effort to control our thoughts will no longer be required; to think quality thoughts becomes the mind's very nature. Until it becomes spontaneous, we must put in constant effort in this direction. In his commentary, Śrī Śaṅkara takes time to point out that if mental discipline is not maintained and one begins ruminating on the various objects and relationships of the world as true and permanent sources of happiness, then eventually the delusion will grow to such an extent that "One may even abuse his guru."[2]

As important as it is to maintain rigorous awareness, discernment and censorship with regards to one's thoughts, one should remember that prior to full assimilation of self-knowledge one can never rid himself of the impulse to view sense objects as a source of happiness. This is also something Kṛṣṇa specifies in the Gītā:

> viṣayā vinivartante nirāhārasya dehinaḥ |
> rasa-varjaṁ rasopyasya paraṁ dṛṣṭvā nivartate ||

> The objects themselves leave the man who doesn't indulge in them, but attachment to their taste remains. Even that taste-attachment turns away from him once he has seen the Supreme.[3]

Here, Kṛṣṇa is saying that, as a spiritual aspirant, even if you avoid indulging in sense objects—*dama*—don't think that you will stop feeling cravings for them. The cravings will continue to some extent, popping up in your mind as impulses from time to time. They will only go once you have fully assimilated and constantly abide in *ātma-jñānam*. Until then, you have to disempower such thoughts continually through discernment.

---

1 Gītā, 2.62–2.63; these verses have been translated in keeping with Śrī Śaṅkara's commentary.

2 gurum api ākrośati

3 Gītā, 2.59

Why is it that only after *ātma-jñānam* becomes firmly assimilated do impulse cravings for sense objects dissolve completely? In his commentary, Śrī Śaṅkara says it is because once we abide steadily in the truth "I am the supreme *brahman*," all of our ongoing sense perceptions become *nirbījam*—seedless. Until then, all of our sensory experiences are constantly registering impressions of either like or dislike. These impressions are stored like seeds in the inner recesses of our mind. When those objects are re-experienced, either through the senses or through memory, those like-and-dislike seeds germinate and the feeling of attraction or aversion arises along with the sensory experience. However, one who firmly abides in self-knowledge has severed the connection between objects and happiness and sorrow. He knows that happiness has only one true source—himself, the ever-present *ātmā*. So, when he experiences the objects of the world, he experiences them as they are, without judging them as attractive or unattractive. Thus, his experience of the world is unsullied by prejudice. As Amma says, "He sees God's creation; not his own creation." Viewing creation and experiences thus produces no such seeds.

In this context, we should explore one more important aspect of the *ātma-jñānī*. On one hand, his mind has been refined—both through his preparatory spiritual practices such as mental discipline and *karma yoga*, as well as through his spiritual understanding regarding his true identity. On the other hand, his understanding regarding his true nature is, of course, that he is not the body and mind but the ever-liberated *ātmā*. He knows that, at best, his true nature serves as the witness to the mind and all its various thoughts, convictions, ideas and emotions, etc. Thus, even though he enjoys a peaceful mind, he knows he is not the mind. This is an important distinction to make because constant mental peace is impossible. The mind is part of the universe—a mixture of energy and subtle matter—and as such it will have fluctuations. We can refine it, of course, but there is no such thing as constant perfect peace at the mental level. *Mahātmās* like Amma have refined their minds to such an extreme extent that we cannot even recognize these fluctuations, but from the perspective of the *mahātmā*, they will be noticed—tiredness will come, a sense of urgency with regard to helping others will come, etc—but the *mahātmā* knows, regardless of the state of the mind, that he is not the mind; he is the eternally peaceful *ātmā*. Thus, while we should never stop disciplining our mind, at a certain point, we also need to start reminding ourselves that ultimate peace is our eternal nature and not something to be attained on the mental level: "I am the ever-blissful *ātmā* despite fluctuations of the mind." This is a step that requires maturity and understanding. If not, we risk becoming like the Vedāntins Amma frequently pokes fun at—people who say, "I am *brahman*," but become angry when tea or food is not brought to them on time.

It is this detachment from the mind and its fluctuations that, in fact, allows for the greatness of *mahātmās* like Amma. For, it is this detachment that creates Amma's capacity to allow her mind to identify with the pain and joy of others, while at the same time remaining totally detached. I remember one time, many years ago, a young man was speaking with Amma. As he was telling Amma his sad story, he began to cry, and as he did so, Amma began to cry as well. Soon the young man was sobbing, and Amma was sobbing also. The look of pain in the boy's face and in Amma's face were almost identical. Seeing Amma weep like this, I thought something terrible had happened and rushed near. Seeing Amma crying, I also started to become upset. Seeing me standing there over the young man's shoulder, Amma suddenly looked at me and—with a totally sober expression—sort of winked, as if to tell me that everything was really okay. (I later learned that he was upset because he felt Amma had not been paying him much attention lately.) Now, the obvious question comes: Was Amma faking? You cannot fake tears like that. You cannot fake that depth of emotion. I am 100-percent positive that Amma's mind was totally identified with the young man's viewpoint and sorrow. However, at the same time, Amma was not identified with her mind. Thus, when interacting with me, Amma was able to switch gears instantaneously—communicate with me—and switch back again. Countless are the examples of this. It isn't only with people's sorrow. Just as often, Amma does the same thing with another's joy. Here, the important thing to understand is that, in her supreme identification with the self, Amma allows her mind to identify with the joy and sorrow of others and yet remains totally detached. This is the ultimate fruit of steadfastness in self-knowledge. At the same time, for Amma—who has come to this world to play the role of the Divine Mother—it is a job requirement! How else could Amma be in the present moment with each individual who comes to her, sharing sorrows one moment, worry the next, excitement thereafter, then joy, then sorrow again? How else would everyone be able to see and experience Amma's total understanding of their mental state and gain strength and courage from that understanding? If Amma were identified with her mind, it would not be possible. As Amma says, "The boat must be in the water, but the water should not be in the boat."

One Who Is of Firm Conviction

DṚḌHA-NIŚCAYAḤ

In fact, Advaita Vedānta is not the only school of Indian spiritual thought, but one of several. While today it is the most prevalent, others still exist. Even within Vedānta, we have not only one theology but several variations—the main three being: Advaita Vedānta, Viśiṣṭha Advaita Vedānta and Dvaita Vedānta.[1] Then there are less-commonly practiced schools of Indian thought as well.[2] In fact, all of these schools accept the Vedas as a *pramāṇam*—a valid source of knowledge.[3] That said, they have all come to different conclusions regarding the Vedic teaching. Added to these are the Pūrva Mīmāṁsakas, who believe that the main point of the Vedas is to instruct us to perform rituals in order to go to heaven after we die. Just as the Advaita Vedāntin's do, the Pūrva Mīmāṁsakas also believe that heaven is ephemeral, but not believing in self-realization, they see temporary sojourns to heaven to be the best deal the universe has to offer. Thus, they advise us to strive throughout our lives to attain as much *puṇyam* [merit] as possible, so that when we die we can spend a few million years in one of the heavenly abodes.

Aside from these six schools, there are six schools of Indian thought that, at least in their canonical doctrines, reject the teachings of the Vedas. One of these is called Cārvāka Darśanam, which boldly

---

1 Advaita Vedānta, consolidated by Ādi Śaṅkaracārya, explains the essence of Vedānta to be a teaching of non-duality, wherein the world and God are understood not to exist as separate entities from their foundation, the ātmā; Viśiṣṭha Advaita, consolidated by Rāmānuja Ācārya, explains a qualified non-duality; and Dvaita, consolidated by Madhvācārya, teaches duality. Each of these three Vedānta systems stresses different statements of the Vedas as being of primary importance, thus bringing out a different import. The primary preceptors of each tradition have written commentaries on the Upaniṣads, Bhagavad-Gītā and Brahma Sūtras.

2 Yoga Darśanam, Sāṅkhya Darśanam, Nyāya Darśanam and Vaiśeṣika Darśanam

3 All six schools accept the Vedas as a valid source of knowledge. However, only Vedānta and Pūrva Mīmāṁsa view the Vedas as the primary source of knowledge and logic as subsidiary. The other four see logic as primary.

proclaims that the only reality is the temporary experiences of the physical body and, therefore, we should base our lives on attaining the maximum amount of pleasure possible.

In Ādi Śaṅkaracārya's time, there was a lot of debate taking place between these various schools of thought. In fact, one of the reasons why Śrī Śaṅkara deserves so much reverence and gratitude is that through his commentaries he pointed out the logical fallacies and scriptural contradictions in the other Indian schools of thought and established the supremacy of Advaita as the ultimate teaching of the Vedas.

When we study Śrī Śaṅkara's commentaries, we see that they are presented in the form of debates with hypothetical proponents of the other schools. These *pūrvapakṣīs* [people of opposing views] present challenges to Śrī Śaṅkara's explanations on the various verses of the scriptures, and Śrī Śaṅkara responds, quelling their doubts and poking holes in their counter explanations as well.

These debates were not entirely hypothetical. During his short life, Śrī Śaṅkara travelled the length and breadth of India and successfully debated renowned scholars of the other schools of thought. In fact, Śrī Śaṅkara gained one of his most ardent disciples in this manner because when he debated the reigning champion of Pūrva Mīmāṁsa—a scholar named Maṇḍana Miśra—he not only defeated him but also inspired him to become his student. Taking *sannyāsa* and changing his name to Sureśvarācārya, Maṇḍana Miśra then proceeded to write a number of important post-Śaṅkara commentaries on the scriptures as well as some original Advaitic treatises, all of which are still studied today.

The reason for explaining all of this is because the next quality listed by Śrī Kṛṣṇa, *dṛḍha-niścayaḥ*, means "one of firm conviction." In his commentary, Śrī Śaṅkara specifies that firm conviction must be there with regard to the *ātma-tattvas*—the principles regarding the self. As people who have attained some degree of spiritual understanding, we may think that we have solid knowledge regarding who we are, but the debates found in Śrī Śaṅkara's commentaries stand as testaments to the fact that there is a lot of room for confusion on the subject of the self. Is the *ātmā* the performer of actions? Is it an experiencer of the fruits of actions? What role does karma play in self-realization? Is there only one *ātmā* or multiple *ātmās*? Is the mind the foundation of the *ātmā*, or is the *ātmā* the foundation of the mind? Is the *ātmā* eternal? If so, what is the proof? Do I have to do something to become the *ātmā* or am I already the *ātmā*? Is there a difference between the bliss of the *ātmā* and the bliss I experience in day-to-day life? If so, what? What is meant when it is said that the *jīvātmā* [the individual self] is one with the *paramātmā* [the supreme self]? Is the *ātmā* all-pervading? Is my *ātmā* the same as the *ātmā* of others? What is meant when we say the world is unreal? Can we experience the *ātmā* and if so how? With the quality "firm conviction," Kṛṣṇa is saying that the *ātma-jñānī* is crystal clear on all of these questions. He has no confusion whatsoever about who he is and what he is not.

We see many Vedāntins that, to some extent, have understood that the consciousness that pervades their own body-mind complex is their true nature. Rarer are those who have truly understood that this consciousness is also the foundation of the world they percieve around them. In essence, they are able to see themselves as divine but are unable to extend that divinity to rest of the world. This shows a lack of clarity, which must be rectified. True clarity with regard to self-knowledge is rare. If that knowledge is truly clear and assimilated, it will express not only in our words, but also in our actions. Most of us know the story of how Amma used to lick the wounds of Dattan, the leper. I remember back then many of us used to tell Amma that she should stop because leprosy was a serious disease, which she could contract. Amma would never listen to us. I remember once, I asked Amma if she wasn't worried that she might fall sick like Dattan? Amma very directly said, "Son, we are not the body. We are the *ātmā*. Whatever is going to happen to the body will happen. That doesn't concern me. I am here to help others." Many people may quote Gītā verses about the indestructability of the self—such as, "Weapons do not cleave it, fire burns it not, water wets it not, nor does the wind dry it"[1]—but how many of them, like Amma, can stand firmly in that conviction in order to uplift others?

Some of the doubts we find expressed by the opponents in Śrī Śaṅkara's commentaries we ourselves may have. Others we may never even have considered. In some ways, "ignorance is bliss," but, in fact, in some situations, until we consider challenging perspectives regarding our true nature and understand why they are fallacious, our understanding will not be firm.

In fact, it is the guru's duty gradually to ensure that the understanding of his disciples is free of all doubts. In order to bring about such firm knowledge, challenging views must be presented to the disciple. This process is referred to in the scriptures as *sthūṇānikhanana nyāya*—the principle of digging the post.[2] This axiom gets its name from an ancient technique of construction, wherein once the foundation posts have been planted, they all must be shaken again and again. In fact it is this intentional shaking that makes them become firm. Only once a post has been rendered firm through this process does it become a fit foundation. Amma says that our understanding regarding our true self must become as clear as our current knowledge regarding our superficial identity. When we wake in the morning, we don't require a refresher to remember who we are, where we live, if we are male or female, etc. Our understanding of our true nature must become just as firm. Studying opposing views and challenges and understanding why they are incorrect can help us to this end.

This practice is not reserved only for *ātma-jñānam*. It appears in many other fields as well. Once a devotee of Amma's had an appointment with a senior doctor who teaches at the Mata Amritanandamayi Math's *āyurveda* college. In the examination room, standing beside the doctor, was the doctor's daughter, who is following in his footsteps. After the devotee discussed his medical problem, the

---

1 Gītā, 2.23: nainaṁ chindanti śastrāṇi nainaṁ dahati pāvakaḥ | na cainaṁ kledayantyāpo na śoṣayati mārutaḥ ||

2 From Śrī Śaṅkara's commentary on the Brahma Sūtras, 3.3.53: "...when the statement of refutation comes after raising the doubt, it produces a firm conviction about the subject matter presented, as per the 'digging the post' axiom."

doctor began suggesting some medicines to his daughter. From his humble manner, one would have thought he was the disciple and the daughter was the master. The daughter nodded as her father listed off the various medicines, but then when he suggested one medicine, the girl said "No, in this situation, that can create constipation, which could further exacerbate the problem." With the same humility, her father softly said, "Oh, right. Then what can we give instead?" To which the girl suggested an alternative medicine. Doubting the doctor's knowledge, the devotee came to me and expressed his concern. He said, "Swāmiji, I am a bit apprehensive about him. He didn't seem very confident when prescribing the medicine." I laughed and told him, "I know that doctor very well. He is one of the most respected doctors in his field. He was feigning ignorance in order to test his daughter and strengthen her knowledge." What a beautiful and systematic teacher-student tradition!

On many occasions I've seen Amma do exactly same thing. In the *āśram*, at least a couple times a week Amma will come to the seashore or main hall for question-and-answer. The majority of time the devotees and disciples ask the questions, and Amma provides the answers. Sometimes, it is Amma who asks the questions and the devotees and disciples who must answer. When this happens, Amma will sometimes really play devil's advocate, making various disciples stand up and clarify their understanding.

"Firm conviction" comes at two levels. If we take the threefold Vedāntic spiritual practices of *śravaṇam*, *mananam* and *nididhyāsanam*, it is the *mananam* stage—wherein we remove our doubts regarding self-knowledge—through which we develop the first level. Here, any confusion or doubt or lack of clarity we had after studying the scriptures is removed. This is level-one "firm conviction." Thereafter, we will likely continue to experience thoughts and impulses that run counter to our Vedāntic knowledge. We need to put in effort to uproot them because only when these contrary thoughts and emotions and habits are eradicated will we experience the full fruit of our understanding. This spiritual practice—*nididhyāsanam*—brings about level-two "firm conviction." Thus, Vedāntic study and clearing our doubts removes uncertainty at the level of the conscious mind, and *nididhyāsanam* helps the knowledge to sink in and gradually saturate the subconscious mind–the origin of thought itself. The tangible mental peace that comes directly from eliminating our negative tendencies should bolster our "firm conviction." It is like successful biofeedback, wherein our mental experience, in its congruity with our intellectual understanding, makes us stand even firmer in our understanding.

As stated in the Introduction, everything depends on our understanding. Thus, firm conviction is essential. In fact, in this regard, we can divide the spiritual journey into four steps. The starting point is ignorance, wherein we only believe in the physical aggregate of matter that is the body and brain. From there, we come to have faith in the concept of soul, but have no real understanding of what that is. Next, through *śravaṇam* and *mananam*, we attain clarity regarding the soul, learning that it is our eternal true nature, etc. However, the journey is not over. From there, through *nididhyāsanam*, we must entrench ourselves in the Vedāntic outlook, gradually uprooting the old thought patterns based upon our old self-conception. Having a clear understanding regarding our true nature is one thing; never losing sight of that understanding or acting contrary to it is another. Only then can we truly be said to have reached the goal as Amma has.

One Whose Mind & Intellect Are Fixed in Me

MAYYARPITA MANO-BUDDHIḤ

The next quality Śrī Kṛṣṇa mentions is *mayi arpita mano-buddhiḥ*—"One whose mind and intellect are fixed in me." Here, we need to understand that when Kṛṣṇa says "me," he does not mean that the *parābhakta* is constantly thinking of Kṛṣṇa with the bluish hue to his skin who plays the flute. When Kṛṣṇa says "me," he does not mean his body and mind. Like the supreme devotee that Kṛṣṇa is describing, Kṛṣṇa is also an *ātma-jñānī*. Therefore, Kṛṣṇa's self-conception is not his body or mind but the *ātmā*—the one and only self of all.

A few years back when Amma was giving *darśan*, a little girl pushed her way up to the side of her chair. The girl told Amma that she wanted to ask a question. Amma smiled and nodded her head in encouragement. She then leaned way over to her right so that the girl could speak directly into her ear. Everyone watched as Amma listened intently, nodding her head each time she registered one of the girl's points. As soon as the little girl finished, Amma told everyone, "She says her father says Amma is Kālī, but her mom says Amma is their mother. She wants to know which one is right!" Amma laughed good-naturedly with everyone, smiling at the girl's innocence. She then gave the girl a peck on the cheek and said, "Do you want to know who Amma is?" The girl's eyes widened, and she nodded, sort of in awe. Amma told her, "If you want to know who Amma is, just know who you are. Then you will know who Amma is." It was a wonderful moment—to the little girl and to anyone who was willing to really listen, Amma was revealing that her ultimate self-conception, her ultimate concept of "I," is not her body-mind complex or even a divine body-mind complex, but the *ātmā*. Moreover, Amma was also revealing that the *ātmā* is not only her true self, but the true self of us all.

A lot of religious conflict has arisen from followers who impose their own limited self-conceptions upon their spiritual leader. The *mahātmā*'s concept of "I" is all-expansive. As already stated by Kṛṣṇa, he is totally devoid of the sense of "mine" and of being a limited, isolated individual. However, many followers of *mahātmās* have limited self-conceptions. Thus, when they hear their spiritual master say "I," they think he is using "I" in the same manner they do—referring to the physical body, mind, name and form. Unfortunately, history is riddled with instances when disciples and devotees have pulled down their guru's concept of "I." As Amma said in the address she delivered upon receiving the James Parks Morton Interfaith Award in 2006, "Due to our ignorance and limited perspective, we are confining *mahātmās* within the tiny cages of religion. In their name, we have locked ourselves inside the prison of the ego, and have proceeded to inflate our egos and fight with one another."

Words mean different things in different contexts, and communication is impossible unless both people involved are using the same definitions. This is why, traditionally, one of the first Vedāntic texts studied is a small treatise called Tattva Bodhaḥ, wherein the basic lexicon of Advaita Vedānta is defined.[1] The idea is that once a student has studied this text, he and his teacher can freely use basic technical terms without either of them having to worry that miscommunication is taking place.

There is a joke that illustrates the importance of establishing common definitions. One winter morning, a husband receives a text from his wife: "Windows frozen. Won't open." The husband texts back, "Pour hot water." Five minutes later the wife texts again, "Computer really screwed up now." So, it's not only in Vedānta, but in all forms of communication that common definitions are important.

If we analyze, we will see that the quality of "having the mind and intellect fixed in the self" has a cause-effect relationship with the previous three qualities. The fixing is the product of being a *yogī*—one

[1] Although commonly attributed to Ādi Śaṅkarācārya, it is probable that Tattva Bodhaḥ was authored by a disciple of Vāsudevendra Sarasvatī, an ācārya in the Kāñcī Pīṭham Śaṅkarācārya guru-disciple lineage.

whose mind has an extremely refined capacity for concentration; of being a *yatātmā*—one whose senses and mind are disciplined; and of having *dṛḍha-niścayaḥ*—firm conviction regarding the nature of the self. The intellect of one who has these three qualities will always be focused on his true nature because such a person enjoys both the knowledge and the mental refinement required for such focus.

Here, we can see that Kṛṣṇa specifies *manaḥ* and *buddhiḥ*—mind and intellect, respectively. While mind and intellect are often seen as synonyms, in Indian spirituality they have different meanings. In fact, Vedānta divides the mind into four faculties: *manaḥ*, *buddhiḥ*, *cittam* and *ahaṅkāraḥ*—the wavering mind, the intellect, the memory and the sense of finite individuality. In Tattva Bodhaḥ, the author provides a traditional definition for *manaḥ*: "the mind is that which is of the nature of conviction and doubt."[1] However, here, when Śrī Śaṅkara glosses the word *manaḥ*, he clips doubt from the definition, writing only, "the mind that is of the nature of conviction."[2] As already discussed, the *jñānī*'s mind no longer holds doubts regarding the nature of God. All such doubts have been resolved during his Vedāntic study under the guru. Thus, by virtue of that fact, his intellect—"which is of the nature of conviction"[3]—is pervaded with the truth of his divine nature. That truth is his intellect's natural place of repose. If he does think of objects, he simply witnesses this process, always remembering that he is not the mind but the consciousness that is its substratum.

Kṛṣṇa says the *ātma-jñānī* will "*always* have his mind and intellect fixed in me."[4] This and similar statements found in the scriptures have led to confusion, primarily the misconception that if one is an *ātma-jñānī* he will always be sitting somewhere with his eyes closed in meditation. Here again we must remember that the *ātma-jñānī* sees everything—all names and forms—as being imbued with the *ātmā*.

---

1 Tattva Bodhaḥ, 7.3.2.2: saṁkalpa-vikalpātmakam manaḥ

2 saṁkalpātmakam manaḥ

3 Tattva Bodhaḥ, 7.3.2.2, niścayātmikā buddhiḥ

4 The word satatam [always], which comes as the second word in Gītā, 12.14, modifies not only saṁtuṣṭaḥ—making it mean "always content"—but all the qualities in the verse. Thus, the verse states the ātma-jñānī is always a yogī, always self-controlled, always of firm conviction, always with his mind and intellect fixed in me.

This understanding serves as the foundation for all of his interactions. Thus, in one regard, even if ostensibly he is thinking of an individual—say, a devotee, a disciple, or even one of his detractors—he is aware that that individual is also himself with a different name and form. As the Gītā plainly says:

> samaṁ sarveṣu bhūteṣu tiṣṭhantaṁ parameśvaram |
> vinaśyatsvavinaśyantaṁ yaḥ paśyati sa paśyati ||
>
> He who sees the Supreme Lord existing equally in all beings, the Imperishable in the perishable, truly sees.[1]

Thus, the Vedāntic vision is not one wherein we think only of the *ātmā*, but one wherein we understand that everything we think about is essentially the *ātmā*.

This is a truth that Amma often highlights in the Kṛṣṇa stories she tells. Even though we think of these stories as "Kṛṣṇa stories," if you pay attention you will see the character Amma is primarily speaking about is not Kṛṣṇa but his devotee Rādhā. Amma glorifies Rādhā by contrasting her attitudes and actions with those of her fellow *gopīs*. Primarily, what separates Rādhā from the others is that where the other *gopīs* are able to see Kṛṣṇa as divine, Rādhā is able to see every aspect of creation as Kṛṣṇa.

It is incorrect to say that we see "instances" or "examples" of this vision in Amma's life because Amma's entire life is verily this vision manifested. Her every action reverberates with the understanding that all beings are divine. People ask Amma, "Do your devotees worship you?" and Amma responds, "No, it is the other way. It is I who worship them."

Since I stand near Amma at the end of her Devī Bhāva programs, I see up close how literally Amma is doing this, throwing handful after handful of flowers upon the devotees who come before her. Although it may be our faith that Amma is blessing the devotees through this action, Amma says she is worshipping them. The flowers she offers upon each person are a form of *pūjā* wherein Amma is acknowledging

[1] Gītā, 13.27

"the Supreme Lord existing in all beings." Note the care with which Amma performs this worship. Despite having given *darśan* for the past 12 or more hours straight, if just one person passes before her without being showered by petals, Amma will stop everyone and call that person back. Amma is living proof that one who has truly assimilated Vedānta sees everything around him—both animate and inanimate—as an embodiment of the supreme self and treats it with love and respect.

One From Whom the World Cowers Not & Who Cowers Not From the World

YASMĀT NA UDVIJATE LOKAḤ LOKĀT NA UDVIJATE CA YAḤ

Śrī Kṛṣṇa next states two qualities in one, saying that the *parābhakta* is both fearless and nonviolent. The line is, *yasmāt na udvijate lokaḥ lokāt na udvijate ca yaḥ*. *Udvijate* means to become agitated, disturbed or afraid. Thus, *yasmāt lokaḥ na udvijate* means, "One of whom the world is not afraid." Similarly, Kṛṣṇa says, *yaḥ lokāt na udvijate ca*–"and one who does not fear the world."

Claims of fearlessness are common these days. Many bumper stickers in the West boldly proclaim "No Fear!" However, can the people who boast such an outlook (if we believe their claims) also say that the world is unafraid of them? There are many bullies, dictators–even psychopaths–who, although they may not be afraid of others, are themselves a source of fear. Thus, Kṛṣṇa specifies that not only is the *ātma-jñānī* unafraid of others, he also does not generate fear in others. He is totally peaceful and nonviolent.

The *jñānī*'s fearlessness is stated categorically not only in several places in the Gītā, but also throughout the Upaniṣads. There, it is explained that the *jñānī*, by nature of his self-knowledge, sees everything in the universe with a vision of oneness–i.e. as ultimately being an extension of his own self. In the individual in whom such a vision has arisen, there is no longer any scope for fear because one does not perceive an "other" of which to be afraid. This truth is beautifully presented in Bṛhadāraṇyaka Upaniṣad in the form of a story involving Prajāpati, the first embodied being. The story goes that, understanding that he was the first being, Prajāpati suddenly understood that he was alone and then, like anyone, became afraid. The story could have ended there, but then Prajāpati thought, "If there is no one but me, of whom am I afraid?" It then says that, with this thought, Prajāpati's fear immediately subsided. The Upaniṣad states the story's real teaching as being the explanation of the phenomenon of fear: *dvitīyād-vai bhayaṁ bhavati*—"Fear arises, indeed, from a second entity."[1] In his commentary on the story, Śrī Śaṅkara elucidates, "Prajāpati's fear was caused only because of ignorance, which cannot exist when one perceives the supreme reality. ... It was quite logical that due to the perception of oneness, his fear vanished. Why? Because fear indeed arises from a second entity. The perception of duality is overcome by means of the perception of oneness because, in reality, there is nothing such as a 'second entity.'"[2]

As discussed before, technically we can say we have "knowledge" once we've fully grasped the Vedāntic teaching regarding our true nature. However, only when we never lose sight of that teaching—and thus every one of our actions, words and thoughts are in alignment with it—can we say that our knowledge is complete. As Amma regularly says, "People have knowledge, but lack awareness." She means many of us have grasped Vedānta but are still incapable of maintaining awareness of its teachings in difficult scenarios and thus fail to consistently think, speak and act in concordance with those truths. Only when we maintain awareness of those truths as we transact in the world will our knowledge truly be bearing its fruit. Until then we will be like the old man who was crying in a bar. The bartender asked him what is wrong and he said, "I have a beautiful young bride at home who is a great cook and thinks I'm wonderful and handsome despite my advanced years." The bartender asked, "What's so bad about that? That's great!" The old man responded, "I can't remember where I live." For knowledge to truly bring us benefit, it must always be available to us when we require it.

There is perhaps no better litmus test for how much we've assimilated Vedānta than fearful situations. Such situations are what

---

[1] Bṛhadāraṇyaka Upaniṣad, 1.4.2

[2] tasya prajāpateryad-bhayaṁ tat-kevalāvidyā-nimittam-eva paramārtha-darśane'nupapanna-mityāha ... | ... | yaccaikatva-darśanena bhayamapanunoda tad-yuktam | kasmāt | dvitītādvastvantarādvai bhayaṁ bhavati tad-ekatva-darśanena dvitīya-darśanamapanītam-iti nāsti yataḥ |

separate people with mere knowledge from people who have fully assimilated that knowledge.[1]

For example, a few years ago, when Amma was in Chennai, a mother and father brought their son for *darśan*. He was a schizophrenic and was shouting and acting extremely violently. In his late twenties, he also looked quite strong. I was standing near Amma at the time, helping with translation from Tamil into Malayalam. The boy was so wild that it took both his parents to properly contain him as they brought him forward for Amma's blessing. As they came closer in the line—I'll be honest with you—I began to feel a little afraid. The father told me, "Swāmiji, we don't know what to do about our son. He's like this all the time. Medicines are not working. Some people even believe he's possessed. He can be quite violent. He has struck his mother and me many times. He even occasionally bites us." By now, the boy was next in line for *darśan*, and my heartbeat was increasing. However, Amma was cool as cucumber. Even after I translated to Amma what the father had told me—that the boy sometimes bites people—Amma was totally relaxed. Here I was, two feet away, full of tension, and there Amma was—with the mouth of an insane man known for biting right against her neck—fully relaxed and blissful. This shows total assimilation of Vedānta.

In fact, tense situations are not uncommon around Amma. When such occasions occur, I sometimes ask Amma about her fearlessness. Whenever I've asked her if she was afraid, Amma has just laughed at me. Once, when I was watching Amma repeatedly put her hand

[1] This is an important concept to understand. Through śravaṇam and mananam—study and clarifying doubts regarding self-knowledge—one is said to become a jñānī. However, vijñānam [perfection in knowledge] comes through nididhyāsanam—the practice of constant effort to uproot habitual thinking that runs contrary to self-knowledge. Thus, while a jñānī may technically know, for example, that he is a non-performer of actions, he may still react in situations with full mental identification with the agent. Only when he has uprooted that habitual identification, can we call him a vijñānī. However, in the Gītā and Upaniṣads, etc, qualifying terminologies such as these are rarely employed. Moreover, different commentators and gurus will use different qualifying terms in their explanations: jñānī, vijñānī; prājñaḥ, sthitaprajñaḥ; jñānī, jñāna-niṣṭha... These are just a few examples. Thus, we can see the importance of studying scriptures under someone competent to help us navigate such passages.

directly inside the mouth of one of the Āśram elephants in order to feed him treats, I asked her if she wasn't afraid. After all, the molar of a full-grown male elephant is about the size of a basketball. Amma chuckled and said, "Son, I don't know what fear is."

Wherever Amma looks she sees only a manifestation of her own self. When one has such a vision, where is the second entity to be afraid of? It is not that Amma doesn't see the birds, the trees, the different people and places. Of course, Amma sees all this, yet she never loses sight of the underlying oneness. She knows that her true nature is pure consciousness and that the entire world around her is nothing but an expression of that consciousness with various names and forms. From another angle, Amma knows that even if the body perishes, the *ātmā* is eternal and can never be harmed.

Unlike with Amma, there is often a very big gap between what we technically "know" and what we feel inside. I remember once, a long time ago, when Amma was still giving *darśan* in a thatched hut, a lady came and told Amma about a problem she was going through. She was not getting along with some of her neighbors. The situation had escalated to the point that they were even threatening her. Amma told her not to be afraid. The woman responded, "No, no, no, with Amma, I'm never afraid! With you in my life, what is there to be afraid of?" The woman then continued to discuss the problem with Amma. The lady was so immersed in her conversation that she did not notice what was happening around her. A long black snake had begun sliding through thatched leaves of the roof. However, the devotees sitting around her did see it, and a couple of them jumped up and started shouting, "Snake! Snake!" At that moment, this woman—who had just professed how Amma's presence in her life had made her fearless—broke free of Amma's embrace and ran to the back of the hut. Amma didn't even get up. As the snake slithered away, she just laughed.

I am not making fun of that lady. In fact, there is nothing wrong with fear. Snakes, elephant molars, psychotic people, etc, indeed can harm us. As such, fear is a natural instinct—a God-given alarm system alerting us to danger and prompting us to act. However, once the instinct has played its role, the fear should leave us and our calm rational mind should quickly return. Fear shouldn't stay with us after it has served its purpose. As Amma said in an address she delivered at the 150th Birth Anniversary Celebrations of Swāmī Vivekānanda in New Delhi in 2013, "Amma is not saying fear is without its purpose. It has a natural and useful function. For example, if a house catches fire, it would be foolish to display fearlessness and stay inside. Amma is only saying that we should not become enslaved by fear."

As stated, the Upaniṣads are emphatic that "Fear arises, indeed, from a second entity." Thus, true fearlessness should only be possible for someone with self-knowledge, who sees the universe as non-different from his own self. However, we often hear of people who are definitely not *ātma-jñānīs* committing seemingly fearless acts. First, we should understand that just because someone risks his life for a given purpose—be it righteous or unrighteous—does not mean that fear is absent from his mind throughout the process. As long as one is not firm in the knowledge that his existence will transcend death, fearlessness is impossible. That said, it is still possible for non-*ātma-jñānīs* to not fear death. This is because there are two levels of self-knowledge—a lower level and a higher level—and even the lower level is capable of making one transcend fear of death.

Lower level self-knowledge is learned from studying the ritualistic portion of the Vedas. For there itself one learns that the soul is eternal, and that one does not really die when the body perishes. In fact, all religions teach this truth. It is the basis of any doctrine involving heaven, hell or rebirth. Yet, we call this "lower level" self-knowledge because the true nature of the soul is still unknown. From the ritualistic section of the Vedas, the self is said to be the performer of actions as well as the recipient of the results of those actions. It is also said to be separate from other souls. In fact, the entire ritualistic section of the Vedas is based on these notions. Therein, one is taught to perform rituals in order to reap the fruit of travelling to heaven, etc. However, when one comes to Vedānta, one learns "higher level" *ātma-jñānam*. Therein the truths about the self that are taught in the ritualistic section of the Vedas are explained to be true only from a relative level of reality. From the ultimate truth, the self is not only eternal but is also one with all other souls and neither a performer of actions nor a recipient of their results.

In fact, level-one self-knowledge is intended to be fear-inducing. For, religious doctrines about heaven, hell and how the fruit of our dharmic and adharmic actions return to us in the form of a just fate—despite being true only from the level of duality—are taught in order to help mankind live a righteous life. Such doctrines induce *bhaya bhakti*—God-fearing devotion—which is religion's initial means of keeping mankind righteous. This is important because, as we see in today's world, people devoid of an incentive for being righteous often embrace adharma. It is dharma that ultimately sustains the world. Without it, this world will fall into total ruin. However, as we mature in life, dharma should become our very nature—not something we practice only out of fear of cosmic retribution. Our life can begin with *bhaya bhakti*, but it should not end there. As Amma says, we need to cultivate proper spiritual understanding and discernment. Once that arises, we will remain steadfast in dharma no matter what happens. In level-two self-knowledge, we learn that, from the ultimate reality of non-duality, the self is neither the agent of any action nor the reaper of the karmic fruit of any action. One might think that this knowledge could bring about adharmic behavior since it reveals that one's actions have no repercussions on one's ture nature. However, by the time we assimilate this truth, we will be mature enough to remain dharmic despite our *bhaya bhakti* having been eradicated by our knowledge.

To understand the origin of the *ātma-jñānī*'s nonviolent and harmless nature, we should return to some of the qualities mentioned at the beginning of the Amṛtāṣṭakam, such as *sarva-bhūtānām adveṣṭā*—"One who has no hatred for any being." Seeing all beings as his own self, the *ātma-jñānī* cannot even think of harming anyone. His only thought is compassion for all. His only prayer is *lokāḥ samastāḥ sukhino bhavantu*—"May all the beings in all the worlds be happy." Furthermore, his inner peace radiates on his face, in his actions and in his demeanor. It is not trapped inside him, as Amma says, "Like honey trapped in a rock." It is there on the surface for everyone to enjoy. People feel naturally at ease with him. Interacting with the *mahātmā*, people know, "This person harbors no selfish motives."

In his commentary, Śrī Śaṅkara specifies that the person being spoken of is a *sannyāsī*–a monk who has formally renounced the world. There are a number of reasons why Śrī Śaṅkara specifies this, which will be discussed later. [See the chapter on Aniketaḥ–One Who Is Homeless.] One reason is that as a part of the *sannyāsī*'s initiation into monkhood, he performs a ritual called *abhāya-dānam*, wherein he formally proclaims to the universe that it has nothing to fear from him. He says three times, *abhayaṁ sarvabhūtebhyaḥ mattaḥ svāhā*–"Let there be fearlessness to all beings from me."[1] The first time he says this addressing all animals, then addressing his fellow man, then addressing the demigods. To the animals, he is saying he will not hunt or eat them or make clothing out them, etc. To his fellow man, he is saying that he will never harm him and, moreover, he won't compete with him over money or jobs or anything else. To the demigods, he is announcing that they also don't have to worry because he won't try to usurp their positions. This is necessary because according to the Vedas, demigods–like Indra, etc–are not fixed entities, but are actually positions won by individuals who have strove for them by performing requisite rituals and austerities. When one takes *sannyāsa*, one vows to cease all actions aimed at bringing pleasure and comfort for himself, including such heavenly attainments. Therefore, the *sannyāsī*'s proclamation that the world need not fear him is not mere lip service. Śrī Śaṅkara knows that only one who has totally renounced material life can completely remove himself from all forms of competition. Thus he stresses that aspect.

Here, it is important to note another aspect of the harmlessness of the *ātma-jñānī*, and that is with regard to the environment. The world is not afraid or disturbed by the *ātma-jñānī* because the *jñānī*, seeing himself as one with creation, can never possibly harm the planet. He takes the bare minimum and gives the maximum. As Amma says, "We should never use more than we require. Today, everyone

[1] Baudhāyana Gṛhya Sūtras, 4.16.4

uses metal spoons, but in olden days we used to create spoons from jackfruit leaves in order to eat *kaññi* [rice soup]. If we take one leaf, it is out of need. However, if we take five or six leaves for ourselves, it is incorrect."

Moreover, a true *ātma-jñānī* can never pollute a river. Seeing every aspect of creation as God, everything as one with himself, he treats every object in this universe with care and love. I remember when we built our *āśram* in Kanyakumari, I also decided to build a hut on the property for Amma. In order to do so, I had eight banana trees cut down. When Amma learned of my actions, she refused to speak to me for three days. Later that year, Amma instructed me to build a school on the property. I had someone draw up the plans. I then told Amma that, in order to build the school, we would have to cut down 35 coconut trees. Amma asked me why, so I showed her the blueprints. The blueprint was the same as had been used for the majority of our schools, with the building taking the form of a straight line. Amma pointed out that all we had to do to save the trees was to change the blueprint into a zigzag formation. It had never occurred to me, but once Amma said it, it was so obvious. In the end not only did we save the 35 coconut trees, I also had 400 more banana trees planted to make up for the eight that I had cut down.

When hearing Kṛṣṇa say that an *ātma-jñānī* doesn't disturb the world, we may get a doubt: There has never been a universally accepted *mahātmā*. Throughout history—from Rāma to Kṛṣṇa to Buddha to Jesus—every enlightened being has had his detractors. It is said Rāvaṇa lived in fear of Rāma, Kaṁsa of Kṛṣṇa, and Herod of Jesus. In Amma's biography, we also read of atheists who were irritated by her as well, even to the point of trying to slander and harm her. Thus, is it really correct to say that the world is not disturbed by the *ātma-jñānī*?

In such cases, fear or irritation is not directly caused by the *jñānī*. It is either a product of the individual's misconceptions regarding the *jñānī*, his jealousy, or due to his fear that the *jñānī* will prevent him from fulfilling adharmic goals. For example, Herod thought Jesus wanted to be king. Jesus was not interested in any such thing. He only wanted to teach mankind that the kingdom of heaven was within—i.e. that they were all already kings. Rāvaṇa's fear of Rāma was steeped in his desire to continue to fulfill his selfish desires through unrighteousness means. He knew Rāma would put an end to that. In essence, the fear is not the fault of the *jñānī* but of his detractor.

It is said that some degree of these qualities is required even before coming to *ātma-jñānam*. As discussed in the Introduction, there is an intrinsic understanding of our oneness at the core of the human psyche. It is that understanding that manifests in the universal values at the foundation of which lies the understanding that one should "Do unto others as you would have them do to you." When we violate such universal values, a rift in our psyche is created, laying the foundation for mental disturbance. A disturbed mind can never hope to assimilate Vedānta. Fear of death and the various vicissitudes of life can be mentally debilitating. As Amma said in her Swāmī Vivekānanda address in Delhi in 2013, "Fear causes our minds to shrink and shrivel. Our mind becomes like a dried-up well. Fear confines our world to a small cell of darkness, like that of a turtle that has withdrawn into its shell upon seeing a predator. It reduces our strength to a tiny speck. We lose our willpower. On the other hand, a fearless mind is as vast as the sky." One with a mind that is like a dried-up well cannot hope to imbibe the subtle principles of Vedānta. How then to gain a certain degree of fearlessness before coming to Vedānta? We have to look to the practice of accepting everything as God's gift.

Along these lines, I've heard a touching story about a husband and wife who were on their honeymoon. They were out in the ocean on a boat. It was a beautiful day and they were enjoying themselves very much. At a certain point the sky clouded. Soon rain began to pour. They started trying to make it back to the shore, but the boat was not very big and did not go very fast. The rain was collecting in the boat. The husband and wife began trying to bail out the boat, the bowline of which was lowering with each gallon of rain that poured inside. Although both were working hard to bail out the boat, the wife still seemed very calm. This irritated the husband. He said, "How are you so calm? Don't you know that this boat could easily sink and neither of us know how to swim?" The wife replied by grabbing a fishing knife from the bottom of the boat and holding it to her husband's neck. Smiling she asked him, "Are you afraid?" The husband responded, "No, of course not." The wife asked why? He said, "Because I know you love me." The wife then said, "That's right. Just as you know the one holding the knife loves you and could never harm you, I also know that the one wielding this storm loves us and could never harm us either."

This is the type of fearlessness possible through faith in God and seeing all as God's gift—the so-called "good" and the so-called "bad." The wife is not saying that they will not drown. She is saying that she has the faith that whatever happens will be God's *prasādam*, and that she knows that God is looking after them and will take care of them as their eternal support. It is a fearlessness based on the "level-one *ātma-jñānam*"—knowing that the soul is eternal. Even though this level of knowledge is incomplete, it can still generate a tremendous amount of courage and peace of mind. Similarly, simply by following dharma we can lead tranquil and non-harmful lives to a great extent.

One Who Is Devoid of Elation, Non-forbearance, Fear & Anxiety

HARṢĀMARṢA-BHAYODVEGAIḤ MUKTAḤ

Next we are presented with some review. Kṛṣṇa says the supreme devotee is *harṣāmarṣa-bhayodvegaiḥ muktaḥ*—one who is free from *harṣaḥ* [elation], *amarṣaḥ* [non-forbearance], *bhayam* [fear] and *udvegaḥ* [agitation].

Freedom from elation was already shown in the chapter on *sama duḥkha-sukhaḥ*—even-mindedness in the face of both negative and positive experiences. Happiness is not a problem, but it should be understood to be our true nature and never the product of any object. For the *ātma-jñānī*, happiness is experienced one of two ways. Primarily it is born out of his knowledge that happiness is his true nature. By virtue of that knowledge alone, he is able to abide in serenity. At the same time, if for some reason a *jñānī* experiences happiness in relation to an object, a situation or an individual, he reminds himself of the fact that the object itself is not the source of that happiness. He maintains awareness that he himself, the *ātmā*, is the very foundation for the entire projected universe, including all its enjoyable objects and the joy that expresses in the mind upon their experience. Amma—who has fully assimilated Vedānta—ever abides in the bliss of the self from the very fact of this understanding. Since there are no desired objects for Amma, there is never an increase in the happiness reflected in her mind upon receiving an object, no matter how desirable that object may seem to others. However, Vedāntins who have yet to fully assimilate self-knowledge will still experience happiness upon the attainment of certain objects, owing to their latent desires for those objects. When that happiness wells up, that Vedāntin must reflect upon its source, reminding himself that it is an expression of his true nature alone.

It should be noted that *harṣa* is not mere happiness. It is extreme elation upon the attainment of an object. Śrī Śaṅkara specifies it to be elation that causes one's hair to stand on end and induces one to shed tears. Such extreme responses to the attainment of objects will never arise for one following the Vedāntic path with alertness. They are only possible for one who remains ignorant of the nature of the objects of the world and of the self.

Amarṣaḥ muktaḥ—freedom from inability to forbear—was previously presented with *kṣamī* [one who forgives, who is patient]. The *ātma-jñānī* knows that change is the nature of the world and that he has no control over how it changes. He has no control over his friends and family. He has no control over his business associates. Some will behave decently; some will behave improperly. He accepts all with a smile, knowing that is how the world is. Amma says that the ability to forbear is required by all people, not just spiritual aspirants. However, the difference between the forbearance of a spiritual person and that of a worldly person is that the former never gives rise to feelings of vengeance. The spiritual person happily accepts everything that comes to him in life. When discussing this quality, Amma points out that this does not necessarily mean that a spiritual aspirant will never experience negative emotions in the face of hardships, but that he will remove them through his discernment. Amma says, "At times, such negative reactions definitely will come, but those with a spiritual outlook will make sure that they invoke their discrimination and, thereby, gradually overcome such negativities. This is the only way to reach our goal. This is why it is so important to develop this quality on the spiritual path."

Really, "elation" and "non-forbearance" are two sides of a coin. When so-called "good" circumstances arise, the *ātma-jñānī* doesn't rejoice; when difficult times come he forbears them with a smile. He knows that both the so-called "good" and the so-called "bad" are part of the ever-changing flux of the universe and thus he takes them in stride. A beautiful quote I recently came across by a Zen Buddhist teacher shows an attitude that can help us become more forbearing: the attitude of seeing every experience as the guru. "Life always gives us exactly the teacher we need at every moment. This includes every mosquito, every misfortune, every red light, every traffic jam, every obnoxious supervisor, every illness, every loss, every moment of joy or depression, every addiction, every breath. Every moment is the guru." This is because every reaction of the mind presents us with an opportunity to reflect upon the spiritual teachings regarding our true nature. What else can you call that but the guru?

Freedom from fear and disturbance was just discussed with the previous quality. However, another point is elucidated by an important post-Śaṅkara commentator.[1] He writes that the distinction between *bhaya* and *udvegaḥ* is that the former is fear that occurs in the face of danger itself—for example, turning the corner and running into a tiger. The latter is tension about the future. Regardless, both are founded on the same principle already discussed, and both are remedied by self-knowledge.

[1] Madhusūdana Sarasvatī, Bhagavad-Gītā Gūḍārtha Dīpikā

One Who Is Devoid of Desires

ANAPEKṢAḤ

Apekṣaḥ means one who harbors desires, expectations, attachments; an *anapekṣaḥ* is one in whom such signs of discontentment and dependence are absent. In his commentary, Śrī Śaṅkara makes sure we understand the extent of the *ātma-jñānī*'s desirelessness. He is devoid of desires and expectations when it comes to sense objects, and also with regard to his own body and sense organs.[1] In essence, *anapekṣaḥ* means someone who knows that his existence is completely independent of the body and mind and whose sense of peace, contentment and happiness are similarly independent of them as well.

When we think of Amma, what do most of us think of? Her fathomless tangible love. To some degree, we have all experienced it—both directly, in Amma's arms, and indirectly, through witnessing how consistently she disregards her own comfort in order to compassionately help those in need. Why is Amma's love so powerful and immense? The reason is her desirelessness—her total independence. Amma's ability to love is so strong because she never bases happiness on the fulfillment of any desire. She knows that peace, happiness and contentment are her true nature. Only when our own inner experience of love is stripped of dependencies can we manifest that love externally in a manner devoid of expectations.

A few years back someone asked Amma about this, specifically how her love was different from that of the love we see in the world. How could Amma say her love was "selfless"? Amma responded, "Because there is no expectation of anything in return. I have no expectations from anyone. So, it is selfless love. Parents bring up their children with love, but that love is mixed with expectations. They think their children will look after them in their old age. There is nothing wrong in that—it is the way of the world—but I don't have

[1] Dehendriya-viṣaya-sambandhādiṣu apekṣa-viṣayeṣu anapekṣo niḥspṛhaḥ—"With regard to the things [most people are] concerned with, such as the body, the senses, the sense objects and their interconnection, etc, he is indifferent—without desire."

such expectations." Then Amma revealed the extent of desirelessness required to love others at her level: "For me, there is no such thing as death. So, I have no fear of death. I live in the present moment and do not think about the future. Other people think about the future. As the child grows up, expectations begin, and the parents begin to become dependent upon their children. But I live on my own. I am totally self-dependent."

In fact, Amma's answer is the perfect commentary on why the *ātma-jñānī* harbors no desires. Just as Śrī Śaṅkara says in his commentary, Amma was saying that one who has fully assimilated self-knowledge doesn't even have any desires with regard to his own body; his happiness isn't connected to the maintenance of his physical health or even his life. Why? Because the *jñānī* knows, "There is no such thing as death."

When Amma says this, it doesn't mean that she believes her body will never die. It means she knows that she is not the body and, therefore, that even when the body dies, she will continue to exist as pure consciousness-existence-bliss. As Amma says, "When a light bulb burns out or a fan stops spinning, it doesn't mean that there is no electricity. When we stop fanning ourselves with a hand-held fan, the flow of air stops, but this doesn't mean that there's no air. Or when a balloon bursts, it doesn't mean that the air that was in the balloon ceases to exist. It is still there. In the same way, the *ātmā* is everywhere. God is everywhere. Death occurs, not because of the absence of the *ātmā*, but because of the destruction of the instrument known as the body. At the time of death, the body ceases to manifest consciousness. So, death marks the breakdown of the instrument, and not any imperfection in the *ātmā*."

The *ātma-jñānī* knows he is not dependent upon the body or mind for his existence. Rather, it is the body and mind that are dependent upon him, the *ātmā*. Moreover, he knows that, as the *ātmā*, bliss is his very nature, regardless of whether or not at any given moment that bliss is reflecting in the mind. This is self-knowledge, and this is why the *ātma-jñānī* is "desireless."

Here a doubt can arise: Doesn't Amma have desires? After all, there is an oft-quoted saying of Amma's that goes:

> "Everyone in the world should be able to sleep without fear, at least for one night. Everyone should be able to eat to his fill, at least for one day. There should be at least one day when hospitals see no one admitted due to violence. By doing selfless service for at least one day, everyone should help the poor and needy. May at least this small dream be realized."

Reading this, how can we say Amma is desireless? When we say "the *ātma-jñānī* is desireless," we need to understand the term properly and from two different levels—the *jñānī*'s mind and the *ātmā*.

From the level of the mind, it doesn't mean that the *jñānī* doesn't have any desires at all, but that his mind doesn't have any selfish desires. Where most people's minds have selfish desires, the mind of the *jñānī* has desires that, when fulfilled, uplift humankind and contribute to the universal harmony. For example, *lokāḥ samasthāḥ sukhino bhavantu*—"May all beings in all the worlds be happy." Moreover, despite having such selfless desires, even if those desires remain unfulfilled, the *jñānī* will not become irritated or depressed. Having nothing to gain for himself, the *jñānī* lives only to uplift humankind, spiritually and materially. Yet, his happiness, contentment and mental peace are eternally independent of whether or not he succeeds in bringing about that upliftment. In this regard I am reminded of Amma's answer to a question someone recently asked her. Reflecting upon all the humanitarian institutions that Amma has started in the past 20 years, this person asked Amma if she was proud of all her achievements. Amma responded, "Son, I am not attached to any of these things. I can go just like that, shedding my skin like a snake. While I am here I am trying to help people; that is all."

Being devoid of selfish desires and not becoming upset if one's selfless desires are unfulfilled is desirelessness from the level of the mind. However, there is another higher perspective from which the *ātma-jñānī* is categorically desireless. Remember, desires are of the mind, and just as the *jñānī* doesn't identify with his body, he also doesn't identify with his mind. Thus he doesn't even see those selfless, unshackling desires as being his desires in the first place. The *ātmā* is of the nature of consciousness. If anything, it can only witness desires, not harbor them—be they selfish or selfless. In fact, it is this higher level of "desirelessness" that allows the *jñānī* to be detached with regard to the fulfillment or nonfulfillment of his selfless desires. As the 14th century Śaṅkarācārya Swāmī Vidyaraṇya states in his classic Vedāntic treatise Pañcadaśī:

> apraveśya cid-ātmānaṁ pṛthak-paśyannahaṅkṛtim |
> icchaṁstu koṭi-vastūni na bādho granthi-bhedataḥ ||
>
> By differentiating the consciousness that is one's true nature from the ego, though [the *ātma-jñānī*] may have millions of desires, there is no harm, for he has severed the knot between *ātmā* and *anātmā*.[1]

If we are honest, most of us will accept that we still have a lot of desires. At the same time, as seekers, we know that if we want to make spiritual progress, we must start eliminating these desires. In fact, one of the main qualifications for coming to Vedānta is at least a relative degree of detachment—*vairāgyam*—and detachment is really no different from being free from desires. The peak of desirelessness—a desirelessness even with regard to one's own health and life—can come only with the understanding and awareness that one is in no way connected to the physical body. If so, how does one begin to cull his mind of grosser desires?

To understand where to begin, we should analyze the various types of desires. We can divide desires into two main types: adharmic desires and dharmic desires. Adharmic desires are unethical: the desire to steal, the desire to harm and kill others, etc. In essence, any desire that violates the Golden Rule of "Do unto others as you would have them do unto you." Removal of such adharmic desires is not only the foundation of becoming desireless but also of becoming just a decent human being. We have to begin there: Any desire the

1 Pañcadaśī, 6.262

fulfillment of which would cheat or harm another being needs to be ruthlessly terminated.

The second type of desire is dharmic desire. These desires are totally normal and righteous: the desire to save money, to have a house, to have clothing, to be healthy, to have a family and to be able to provide for that family, to have a good job, etc. There is nothing wrong with such desires, but we have to be careful with them. Our entire life should not be dedicated solely to their fulfillment. Thus, when it comes to the proportion of our mental and physical activity occupied by such desires and their fulfillment, we must be alert. As spiritual aspirants, we need to make sure that we leave adequate time for spirituality—for helping others, for social service, for doing our meditation, *arcana* and *japa*, for studying the scriptures and guru's teachings, etc. In 2006, in the address Amma delivered on her 53rd birthday, Amma gave a nice example that illustrates this point. She said, "Pursuit of dharma, wealth, pleasure and liberation are said to be the four pillars of life. In today's world, awareness of dharma is being lost. The desire for liberation is also in decline. What remains are only the pursuit of money and pleasure. Thus, today's society is like a car with its front tires gone flat. For real progress to take place, the pursuit of money and pleasure are not enough." The front tires of the car are the ones that turn and thus dictate the direction of the car. In comparing dharma and liberation to the front tires, Amma was pointing out that that the pursuit of money and pleasure should always remain subservient to these two higher goals. Thus it is important to ensure that the pursuit of money and pleasure—even if within the confines of dharma—never come at the expense of one's pursuit of liberation. Ensuring this is the second level of desire control.

The foundation of pruning the mind of adharmic desires is to understand why they are harmful to us. We should understand and ruminate on the fact that the damage caused to our psyche by violating dharma always outweighs any potential material benefit. Since the psychological ramifications of engaging in unrighteousness are not always immediate, this foundational understanding must be clear. Only then will we become alert when adharmic desires enter our mind. In fact, the conscience is a God-given alarm system. Its prick is alerting us to the fact that what we are doing or are about to do is detrimental to our psyche. The more we refine our mind, the stronger this alarm system will become. However, the more we ignore this alarm, the quieter it will become. Eventually, we will not even hear it. When the alarm system burns out completely, it is difficult to repair. So, we must be careful.

Cultivating this discernment is crucial for removing unrighteous desires. However, the process doesn't end there. We all have had the experience of knowing something is wrong but doing it anyway. Thus, we also must cultivate *śamaḥ* [mental discipline] and *damaḥ* [sensory discipline]. Mental discipline is the ability to change the direction of our thoughts when adharmic desires arise—to flip the mental channel, as it were. Sensory discipline is the practice of avoiding the very people, places and situations, etc, that trigger our latent desires in the first place. [For more on these disciplines see the chapter on Yatātmā.]

What about our desires that are not against dharma but at the same time are materialistic? How do we ensure they do not get out of hand? We have to live a life of reflection. We have to cultivate awareness regarding where our life is headed and how our goals are changing. We have to bring back to our awareness that the fulfillment we are seeking can never come from such desires. The fulfillment they seem to offer is like the horizon; no matter how far you walk toward it, that much it will recede. Furthermore, we must remind ourselves that as much temporary happiness we allow ourselves to take from them, that much sorrow they will eventually cause us. Discerning thus, we can ensure that our life remains balanced and that we don't lose sight of the spiritual goal. Then, with the dharmic materialistic desires we do retain, we can cultivate an attitude of acceptance. If we can offer our efforts to fulfill them as worship and accept their fulfillment and nonfulfillment alike as God's *prasādam*, we will thereby disempower them of their ability to disturb our peace of mind.

Up to this level of desire control, Vedānta is not required. However, for the final stage it is absolutely necessary. The final stage is becoming like Amma—one whose only desires are selfless and whose peace, happiness and contentment are in no way associated with the fulfillment of those desires. As discussed, our desires only become totally selfless through understanding that our existence and happiness are in no way dependent upon the body-mind complex. Moreover, the peak of desirelessness comes when we sever our identification with even that selfless desirer: "Let the mind have millions of selfless desires! I am not the mind; I am the ever-detached and blissful consciousness. If they are fulfilled fantastic; if they are unfulfilled, that is also fine." Such a level of spiritual perfection can only come through studying and assimilating the truths taught to us by the scriptures and guru.

One Who Is Pure

ŚUCIḤ

The next characteristic of the supreme devotee is *śuciḥ*—one who is pure. Śrī Śaṅkara clarifies, "One who is endowed with both external and internal purity."[1] External purity not only refers to the purity of our surroundings and of our physical body but also to the purity of our conduct—how we talk and act. Internal purity is referring to the purity of our mind—our thoughts, emotions and attitudes. Thus, Śrī Kṛṣṇa is saying that the *ātma-jñānī* would not only unhesitatingly welcome impromptu inspections of his home, but also of his mind.

In the old days, when Amma's time wasn't totally occupied with *darśan*, Amma would regularly come to the various huts and *seva* departments for unannounced inspections. I remember one such kitchen inspection. Amma looked in one place, then another, checked the dust on the shelves, checked the garbage pails for excess waste. Everything looked good, and all the *brahmacāriṇīs* doing *seva* there sighed in relief. Then, suddenly, Amma walked over to a big pot sitting in the corner. When she went to lift it, her hands came away covered in soot. She then pointed out that the same pot had been sitting there unwashed since the last time she had inspected the kitchen. "Two weeks back I saw this pot but didn't say anything because I wanted to see if any of you would wash it without being asked. This shows your lack of *śraddha*[2]. If any of you had any *śraddha*, you would not have left it sitting here like this. A person without *śraddha* is unfit to be a spiritual seeker. Lack of *śraddha* externally will lead to lack of *śraddha* internally as well."

The worst thing about Amma's surprise inspections is that when she finds something dirty, she will almost always clean it herself without letting anyone help her, which she did on this occasion as well.

---

[1] bāhyena abhyantareṇa ca śaucena sampannaḥ

[2] In Sanskrit, śraddhā means faith, but in Amma's language of Malayalam it primarily means alertness, care and attention to detail.

As Amma pointed out, maintaining the cleanliness of one's environment and body is the foundation of all purity. One who cannot keep his grossest aspects clean has little hope of doing so with the subtlest.

Here, we may get a doubt. In Amma's biography, we read that there were times when she totally ignored external purity. She would go without bathing. She would eat things like fish dropped from the talons of kites. She would even sit in the bog of the backwaters lost in meditation. When we read of such incidents, we should understand that Amma did not do any of these things intentionally. Her disregard to her cleanliness was due to her being lost in the bliss of the self. Such spontaneous disregard for one's surroundings and physical condition may come for one who has attained *ātma-jñānam*. In some rare cases, it can also happen for a seeker who has become one-pointed in his spiritual practices. Thus, if it comes without our awareness as a result of our devotion, it is acceptable, but never as a planned course of action or from neglect. We should never think, "I am a spiritual aspirant; let me not waste time bathing or cleaning." Such thoughts are almost always born of laziness. If you are a spiritual aspirant, then take it as a spiritual practice to clean yourself and your environment.

We should not think that external purity ends with physical cleanliness. Even if we take three baths a day and our house looks like something out of *Better Homes & Gardens*, if our behavior is foul, then we have yet to attain external purity. Thus, "external purity" also means that the *ātma-jñānī* is always a pleasant person, ever helpful and kind, with sweet words always at the ready, quick with a smile and a hand. That said, we all know people who externally are extremely kind but who secretly are cursing anyone and everyone. They may have some degree of external purity, but internally they are still a mess. So, by saying "internal purity," we mean that there is no such duplicity in the *jñānī*. His kindness and good character are not a mask but are his true face.

Although in some extreme exceptions external cleanliness may be absent in the *ātma-jñānī*, there are no exceptions with regard to internal cleanliness. Mental purity will be found even in the most unorthodox of *avadhūtas*[1]. What is mental purity? A mind devoid of animosity, jealousy, greed or any other thought, emotion or attitude incongruous with self-knowledge. Negative emotions and attitudes are rooted in erroneous perceptions regarding our own true nature or the true nature of the world. Thus, they cannot exist in one who has clear understanding. As Amma often points out, "How can one who truly understands that the 'I' in me is the 'I' in him, ever become jealous or angry at another person?"

In the end, it is self-knowledge that is the ultimate purifier. This is something that Kṛṣṇa emphatically states in the Gītā: *na hi jñānena sadṛśaṁ pavitram-iha vidyate*—"Indeed, there is no purifier here comparable to knowledge."[2] He says this because it is our understanding of something that dictates our attitude toward it, and our attitude that dictates our thoughts, words and actions. Thus, our understanding regarding our nature, the nature of the universe, and the nature of God is the final fire that burns away all the dross aspects of our personality.

At the same time, a relative degree of purity is required even for coming to *ātma-jñānam*. How can we bring this purity about? Obviously, *ātma-jñānam* is not required for keeping our body and environment clean. It is also not required for behaving properly. We all know many extremely decent people who have never even heard of Vedānta; some of them may even be atheists. Even mental purity, in terms of dulling the effect of our likes and dislikes and reducing negative emotions, can be brought about by *karma yoga* and other spiritual practices. Thus, when Kṛṣṇa says that knowledge is the ultimate purifier, he is really saying that no other spiritual practice can remove the *ahaṅkāra*. *Ahaṅkāra* is the impurity that pollutes our concept of "I" with the idea that we are a limited individual who is both the performer of actions and the enjoyer of their results. In fact, it is this impurity with regard to "I" that makes us feel disconnected from God as well as from other beings. As we said before, "I" is

1 An ātma-jñānī who, for whatever reason, does not conform to social or scriptural norms.

2 Gītā, 4.38

not the problem; the problem is our distorted concept of "I." As our distorted concepts are all founded on ignorance, they can only be rectified through knowledge.

One Who Is Efficient

DAKṢAḤ

Just as some people have the misconception that, due to the mind reveling in the self, a devotee will be loose with cleanliness and order, so too some people believe he will be inefficient and sloppy with regard to his actions. Just as Śrī Kṛṣṇa negated the former with *śuciḥ* [purity], now he negates the latter with *dakṣaḥ*. *Dakṣaḥ* means one who is efficient, capable, skillful. With this quality, Kṛṣṇa is saying, that as life unfolds and its various issues present themselves, the *jñānī* quickly sees to the heart of each matter, ascertains what is and isn't required and acts, or doesn't act, accordingly.

When the Indian Ocean tsunami hit the coast of Kerala in 2004, no one expected it and there was no precedent. Yet, within minutes, Amma herself was down in the floodwaters, calling all the shots. She sent one group of people to get all the boats on the peninsula for ferrying people across the backwaters to safety. She sent another group to start shifting the soaked 40-kilogram sacks of rice from the kitchen to the college, which she immediately decided would become a refugee camp. She sent another group to evacuate the elderly and invalids from the Āśram's charitable hospital. She told the person in charge of the International Office to bring all the foreigners' documents across. She sent another group to go look in the area surrounding the *āśram* for people who may be injured. Aware of the fact that if family members didn't cross the backwaters as a group, it could take them days to locate each other, Amma made people wait until they found everyone in their family before allowing them to enter a boat. Knowing another wave could come, Amma even sent the *āśram* cows and elephants into the temple hall, the floor of which is an extra 15-feet above sea level. Amma's mind was like a supercomputer working at top speed, constantly assessing, evaluating and setting people and things into motion. Since the tragedy, many senior officials who work in disaster management have asked Amma about the decisions she made that day. They have all wanted to know from where her brilliance and skill in action came? How did she manage to think of so many subtle aspects? When one such official asked Amma, she responded, "For me, there is no planning; everything just comes spontaneously." How is this possible?

As part of a traditional study of Vedānta, one also studies *tārka śāstra*—the science of logic. As per Vedāntic logic, the mind has six *pramāṇams*—or valid means of knowledge. These are *pratyakṣa*—knowledge born of sensory perception; *upamāna*—knowledge gained through comparison; *anupalabdhi*—knowledge gained through non-perception; *anumānam*—knowledge gained through inference; *arthāpatti*—postulation; and *śabda*—knowledge of facts gained through the Vedas and other testimonies. Without going into detail, these are the various means for the mind to learn and think. For example, I see smoke on a mountaintop and I think, "There must be fire up there." This is a form of inference. In fact the mind is running a process: "I see smoke coming from the top of that mountain. Whenever I have seen smoke in the past, there has been fire. Therefore, there must be fire on the mountaintop now." In a refined mind, such processes take place in the blink of an eye, automatically and naturally. According to the logic texts, all the data we gain is from either sensory perception or testimony (scriptural and worldly), and all the various conclusions we draw regarding that data are derived via the mental processes that are the other four *pramāṇams*.

All of us have minds. Some of us have supercomputer minds and some of us seem to be using an outdated operating system. Why is the *ātma-jñānī*'s mind so quick? Why is he able to see every situation as it truly is and, as if punching a calculation into a machine, come up with so many solutions? The answer is simple: His mind is totally refined and all these mental processes are able to work at full efficiency. In fact, it is the previous quality of mental purity—including the ultimate mental purity that comes via self-knowledge—that has made him so efficient. Remember, through meditation, the *jñānī*'s mind has been made capable of laser-like focus. Through *karma yoga*, his mind has been stripped of distractions in the form of likes and dislikes. And, finally, through his study of Vedānta, he has attained the knowledge that he himself is the source of all happiness. Thus, his mind is no longer goaded by thoughts aimed at trying to find happiness in external objects. Moreover, he understands that all material phenomena are but superficial names and forms that have risen from the eternal substratum of the self. Thus, he is no longer limited by anxiety and fear. What remains is a spiritual educated mind that is fully available to apply itself to whatever situation may be at hand. Such a mind absorbs the data presented to it and runs all the various analytical processes and comes up with various solutions at lighting speed.

One Who Is Impartial

UDĀSĪNAḤ

Udāsīnaḥ means one who is impartial. The *ātma-jñānī* views all the various aspects of the world—its people, places and things—as his own self appearing with manifold temporary names and forms. As Amma says, "In the same way that everyone knows that the necklace, the earring and the bangle are all nothing but gold, one who understands the ultimate truth of this universe knows that everything he sees is God." In the fifth chapter of the Bhagavad-Gītā, there is an oft-quoted verse presenting this vision:

> vidyā-vinaya-saṁpanne brāhmaṇe gavi hastini |
> śuni caiva śvapāke ca paṇḍitāḥ sama-darśinaḥ ||

> Men of learning see with equal vision a brāhmaṇa endowed with knowledge and humility, a cow, an elephant, a dog, even a dog-eater.[1]

When viewing the world through this ultimate perspective—in which name and form, and all qualities good and bad, are discarded as superfluous—how can the *ātma-jñānī* favor one person over another?

When explaining *udāsīnaḥ*, Śrī Śaṅkara, specifically notes that the *ātma-jñānī* doesn't favor any friends.[2] Why? Because, as Kṛṣṇa has already said at the outset of the Amṛtāṣṭakam, the *ātma-jñānī* is *sarva-bhūtānāṁ maitraḥ*—a friend to all beings. Therefore, when there is an argument or competition, it is not really that he doesn't favor his friends but that—seeing both parties as his friends—he wants the best for both. Along these lines, sometimes before governmental elections people will ask Amma if she is going to vote. Amma always says, "If I were allowed to vote for each candidate, then I would vote. I am a mother. How can a mother choose one child over another?"

---

[1] Gītā, 5.18

[2] na kasyacid mitrādeḥ paksaṁ bhajate yaḥ sa udāsīnaḥ

The fact is, Amma sees everyone as a divine extension of her own self. When viewing the world through this perspective, anyone will have difficulty taking sides. I remember once, in the early days of the Āśram, we were having problems with a thief. Small things kept disappearing from here and there, even some money. Either the thief was very clever or we were easily tricked because weeks went by without anyone being able to catch him. Then, finally, one of the *āśram* residents spied the culprit in the act. It was a young boy from one of the nearby houses, about 10. He tried to run but was caught. The *āśram* resident tied the boy's hands behind his back with a cloth and brought him to Amma. However, when Amma saw him, she just closed her eyes in meditation. We waited, but Amma showed no signs of stirring. In the end we just let the boy go. When Amma did open her eyes, I asked her why she had entered such a sublime state upon seeing the boy. Amma said, "Seeing him standing there with his hands behind his back reminded me of Śrī Kṛṣṇa."[1]

Don't get the wrong idea. Just because, in this particular instance, Amma decided to view things from a transcendent perspective, doesn't mean that *mahātmās* cannot take decisions in the day-to-day world. Even in this circumstance, Amma was in fact making a decision because, despite being let off the hook, the boy never stole from the *āśram* again. Amma knew that he had learned his lesson and there was no need to involve his parents or the village authorities. The *mahātmā*'s impartiality doesn't limit his ability to make decisions. After all, Kṛṣṇa has just said the *jñānī* is *dakṣaḥ* [efficient] with regard to the various matters that arise before him. The supreme perspective of seeing all as the self only explains why the *mahātmā* cannot favor one person over another in the same way that a father will favor his son over his neighbor's son, etc. The *ātma-jñānī* definitely perceives the relative world, and he does indeed know that, from the relative perspective, there is a difference between a learned and humble person and a cruel person with no culture. He does know that there is a difference between an elephant, a cow and a dog, etc. It's just

[1] In his youth, Kṛṣṇa often would steal butter from his fellow villagers. Once, to make him stop, his stepmother, Yaṣoda, tied his hands behind his back.

that he never loses sight of the substratum of these various beings. Just because we know the necklace, earring and bangle are all gold doesn't mean that we become confused about which part of the body they are designed to adorn.

So, how does the *mahātmā* make decisions? For this, he only has one means of evaluation. Not "With whom do I share more blood?" Not "With whom do I have more in common?" Not "With whom do I have stronger business/political ties?" But only "Who is aligned with dharma? What should be done from that perspective?"

In fact, the majority of people know that impartiality is a virtue to which they should adhere. However, they are overpowered by their attachments and desires and thus find that, despite knowing they are being partial, they cannot act otherwise. By power of his knowledge, the *jñānī* has transcended such attachments and is able to think, speak and act in accordance with universal laws of righteousness.

Actually, the quality of impartiality sheds new light on the previous quality of *dakṣa* [efficiency] as well. This is because it reveals to us another area in which the *jñānī* is efficient. That area is with regard to knowing when he should view a situation from the "supreme perspective" wherein all is seen to be the self, and when he should view a situation from the "transactional perspective," wherein the relative differences come into the foreground.[1] In fact, developing discrimination with regard to this is a subtle, but crucial, aspect of spirituality. Many people have trouble negotiating this, despite being longtime spiritual aspirants. The result can often be rather comedic.

I will give you an example that took place several years ago during Amma's North India Tour. Amma was conducting three days of programs at her *āśram* in Bangalore. Just outside the *āśram*, there is an enormous banyan tree that has been there for so long that it has become both a place and object of worship for the local villagers. In the unique vision of India, the tree is both temple and God at the same time. After Amma's tour group arrived, one devotee, about 20 years old, saw the tree in the distance and decided to walk to it. When he

[1] These perspectives are referred to in the scriptures as the paramārthika dṛṣṭi and the vyāvahārika dṛṣṭi, respectively.

reached the tree, he tangibly experienced the purity of its environment and decided to sit down and chant the Lalitā Sahasranāma. After chanting 100 names or so, he decided that he wanted to climb the tree and sit peacefully on one of its branches as he completed his *arcana*. So, he did. Fortunately or unfortunately, the villagers saw him sitting there—sitting atop their temple, their God—and came running over and started shouting at him. The young man didn't understand why they were so upset, so, he just kept on chanting. That is when the rocks started coming at him, which of course did the trick.

Later, the whole story was related to Amma. The young man told Amma, "I don't understand. Everything is God. Not just the tree. Even the sandals on these people's feet are God, but they don't feel it's offensive that they are standing on them!"

Amma told him, "That's right, son. Everything is God. But just because fire is God, would you sit in it? Urine is also God, but would you urinate on a religious symbol?"

Amma was reminding him that just because everything is the all-pervasive divine self doesn't mean that we stop conforming to social and practical norms. Open the symbolic third eye of unity, but don't close the two normal eyes of duality. When you close your eyes in meditation, let duality fall away and appreciate everything as one. When you go about your daily affairs, let duality be in the foreground, while maintaining your non-dual understanding in the background. Otherwise, you will make a mess of life.

One Who Is Free From Emotional Pain

GATAVYATHAḤ

The next quality stated by Kṛṣṇa is *gatavyathaḥ*. In this context, *vyathā* means emotional pain. *Gatavyathaḥ* means a person whose heart has become incapable of being emotionally hurt. Moreover any emotional scars that were once there have also been debrided through the power of his self-knowledge.

Total emotional resilience is only possible when we become capable of fully accepting everything that happens in life—events in the past, events in the present and events in the future. It is in fact the boundaries that we set up in order to protect ourselves emotionally—boundaries in the form of "I" and "mine"—that expose us to potential emotional injury. The boundless heart cannot be wounded for it has no such fortifications. In its inclusion of everyone and everything, it leaves nothing outside to assail it. Thus, the *ātma-jñānī* has no expectations with regard to the relationships in his life. He knows that everyone in this world will act according to his own nature, and he therefore accepts praise and criticism, fondness and antagonism, and success and failure as the nature of life. He doesn't even harbor any expectations with regard to his own body or mind. He accepts everything that comes, knowing that it is but the ebb and flow of the transitory reality we refer to as the universe. When hardship comes his away—as it does for everyone in this world—he stands detached from his own maltreatment, even his persecution, as if watching a film. As Amma always says, "He lives in the world detached, like butter floating on the surface of water."

How many people during the past 60 years have attacked or ridiculed Amma? How many names has she been called by the ignorant and petty? How many times has she been attacked physically? How many people who once told her that they want to dedicate their lives to her and her charitable mission have changed their minds—some even turning their back on her? Of course, Amma has never asked anyone to make such pledges. My point is only that Amma has faced more adversity than most people face in 1,000 lives, but none of it has ever dulled her shine, even for a moment. It has never made her depressed. It has never caused her to bear ill will toward anyone. It has never made her stop helping people or seeing everyone as her beloved child.

Last year, during one of Amma's question-and-answer sessions in Amritapuri, someone asked Amma how she was able to endure all the difficulties she experienced in her youth. Amma responded, "An awareness of my own true nature as well as the true nature of the world was always with me. Established in these principles, it was always clear that the supreme self is the only thing that can ever provide real strength and support. The love we experience from the world is always tinged with selfishness; it is temporary."

If we reflect, we will see that all of our emotional wounds have come because of some expectation. We expect someone to be there and love us forever, and they leave us. We expect someone to be honest with us, and they lie to us. We expect someone to treat us with respect, and they ridicule us in front of others. The majority of people live not in the real world but in a world fashioned in the form of their expectations. Tragically, expectations make for a fragile edifice, and when that scaffolding breaks, the world we were living in falls apart and we become injured emotionally. Therefore, the *jñānī* understands that anything can happen to him or to his friends and relations at any moment. He lives with that awareness. At the same time, he remembers that he—in his true nature—is not in any way dependent on the world. In this way, not only is he not surprised when adverse situations and failures arise, he is also emotionally at peace throughout the process. He knows that everything that happens in the world—the so-called "good" and the so-called "bad"—is but a mere drama. He simply watches this drama unfold upon the screen of the supreme consciousness that is his true nature.

Amma often points out that our emotional scars bind us, like prisons. Therefore, it is in our best interest to confront them and put in the effort to change our thinking regarding the issues that created them. Until we do so, self-realization will remain a distant dream. Why? Because each emotional scar is an indicator that we are still identifying with the body and mind, that we are still claiming people, places and things as "mine," that we still believe we have the right and power to control aspects of creation. All such attitudes are antithetical to self-knowledge, which says "I am neither the body nor the mind; I have no possessions, no relationships, no powers or rights to control people and situations. I am the bliss that is ever apart, the peaceful witness consciousness. As such, I accept everything within and without, totally devoid of expectations."

One Who Has Renounced All Undertakings

SARVĀRAMBHA PARITYĀGĪ

Śrī Kṛṣṇa now says that the *parābhakta* will be a *sarvārambha parityāgī*—one who has renounced all undertakings. The concept that spiritual life culminates in the rejection of actions is difficult to understand. We will investigate this in more detail with the upcoming quality of *śubhāśubha parityāgī*—one who renounces both the auspicious and inauspicious. With the quality at hand, we will limit the *ātma-jñānī*'s renunciation of action, as per Śrī Śaṅkara's commentary, to "the renunciation of actions undertaken out of desire for the purpose of enjoying the fruit, here or hereafter."[1]

In the context of the periods of time when Śrī Kṛṣṇa and Śrī Śaṅkara lived, this quality specifically refers to the cessation of Vedic rites aimed at material gain, known as *kāmya karmas*. When we look at the ritualistic portion of the Vedas, we see that it is full of such rites. Some of those rituals are for attaining such benefits while we are still living this current life—for example, rituals for a spouse, a child, money, long life, etc. Other rituals are aimed at attaining material gain after we die—specifically sojourns to heaven or becoming a demigod. While the latter goals may initially sound spiritual to us, if we contemplate we will see that they are purely material in nature. Despite being "otherworldly," they are very much "worldly." What is heaven but a superior house with superior neighbors? What is becoming a demigod but gaining a superior body and mind? The Indian spiritual tradition says that none of these have anything whatsoever to do with spirituality, which is abiding blissfully in our own true "spirit," the

---

[1] ihāmutra-phala-bhogārthāni kāma-hetūni karmāṇi sarvārambhāḥ tān parityaktuṁ śīlam asya iti sarvārambha-parityāgī—"Sarvārambhāḥ means works undertaken out of desire for the purpose of enjoying the fruit here or hereafter. He who is apt to give them up is a sarvārambha parityāgī."

eternal self. Thus, here, Kṛṣṇa is saying the *jñānī* will categorically cease performing any such rites.

In today's day and age, very few people perform any rites—Vedic or non-Vedic—at all, be they selfish or selfless. Thus, we can expand the meaning of this statement beyond the confines of Vedic rites to mean that the *jñānī* will cease any action aimed at attaining for himself pleasure, comfort or security. The reasons for this have been discussed at length already, but are perhaps best summed up by Kṛṣṇa himself

> yāvān artha udapāne sarvataḥ saṁplutodake |
> tāvān sarveṣu vedeṣu brāhmaṇasya vijānataḥ ||
>
> To an enlightened brāhmaṇa[1], all the Vedic rites are as useful as a water-tank when there is a flood everywhere.[2]

Kṛṣṇa is saying, when we have realized our own true nature to be the very source of all experiential bliss, why would we perform any ritual for the purpose of experiencing happiness through material gains? In fact, why would we perform any action—be it religious or mundane—to achieve such an end?

The devotees and disciples of Amma are very much aware of how much strain she puts on her physical body. This lifestyle of hers, wherein nothing is ever done with a self-serving motive, can be rather frustrating for us. We want Amma to take a break and do something that we would consider relaxing. Yet, Amma is not interested. I remember a few years back one devotee came for *darśan* and said, "Amma, why can't you take a vacation? Perhaps you could go to Hawaii and relax on the beach. We devotees would pay for it, and you could rest your body for a week or so."

Laughing and giving the man a compassionate smile, Amma answered, "You have a son. If he were sick or sad or needed you, would you be able to just take off and go to the beach? Of course not.

---

[1] In this context, brāhmaṇa does not refer to one born into a specific caste, but one of a disciplined and refined mind.

[2] Gītā, 2.46

You would stay with him. This is how it is with Amma. All are my children, and I cannot leave them to take some vacation."

Having understood his own self to be the essence of all peace, the *jñānī* is eternally at rest. Thus he harbors no motive to perform any action to attain peace, comfort or any other form of happiness.

One Who Neither Rejoices, Hates, Grieves Nor Desires

YAḤ NA HṚṢYATI NA DVEṢṬI NA ŚOCATI NA KĀṄKṢATI

Next, Śrī Kṛṣṇa elaborates on a quality he has already mentioned in the first verse of the Amṛtāṣṭakam with *sama-duḥkha-sukhaḥ*—one who has mental equipoise in both hardship and favorable circumstances. Since we have seen this before, we can simply note, as Śrī Śaṅkara points out, that when Kṛṣṇa says *na hṛṣyati*, it means the *ātma-jñānī* does not rejoice upon attaining an object most people enjoy, and *na dveṣṭi* means he does not feel aversion about receiving an object most people detest. Similarly, *na śocati* means he does not grieve upon losing a favored object. *Na kāṅkṣati* means, "He does not desire anything unattained."

The *ātma-jñānī* knows the peace that is his true nature can never be affected by the material objects of the world. At most he see his body's interaction with the various objects as a play to which he is a spectator. Even more wondrous is his understanding that "This play—with all of its colors, shapes, variations, comedic aspects, tragic aspects, adventure and uneventful moments—has only one thing as its foundation, and that is me—pure consciousness. Even the duration of the play—the principle of time itself—is but an illusion to which I am serving as the substratum." For one with such a view of himself and the cosmos, where is the scope for elation, hatred or grief? What is there even to desire?

One Who Has Renounced the Auspicious & The Inauspicious

ŚUBHĀŚUBHA PARITYĀGĪ

With the quality before last, Śrī Kṛṣṇa said the *parābhakta* was a *sarvārambha parityāgī*, which Śrī Śaṅkara explained as meaning he has ceased performing rituals and actions aimed at attaining happiness through objects. Now Kṛṣṇa takes things a step further saying that the *jñānī* will be a *śubhāśubha parityāgī*—one who has renounced not only selfish actions, but action altogether, be it auspicious or inauspicious.

The idea that spiritual life culminates in the cessation of all actions is difficult to grasp. As such, many people misunderstand such statements. Then, in their confusion, they either write them off as impractical or escapist, or they embrace their mistaken understanding of them and become good-for-nothing. Kṛṣṇa himself warns that many spiritual seekers are confused on this issue. He tells Arjuna: *kiṁ karma kim-akarmeti kavayo'pyatra mohitāḥ*—"Even scholars are deluded with regard to what is action and what is inaction."[1]

Fortunately for us, Kṛṣṇa himself clarifies. He says that when an *ātma-jñānī* "renounces karma," it does not mean that his body and mind cease to perform actions—i.e. he ceases to move, to speak and to think. On the contrary, the *ātma-jñānī*'s body may move, speak and think much more than that of the average person. To confirm this, one only has to take the three primary examples cited in this book: Śrī Kṛṣṇa, Śrī Ādi Śaṅkarācārya and Amma. Śrī Kṛṣṇa actively played the roles of son, cowherd, disciple, king, husband, servant, guru and friend—all of which involved copious interaction and action. He battled Kaṁsa, Kāliya and Narakāsura, lifted Govardhana Hill, served as charioteer to Arjuna in the Mahābhārata War and, of course, taught Arjuna the wisdom recorded as the Bhagavad-Gītā. Likewise, Śrī Śaṅkara, even though he was a *sannyāsī*, authored elaborate

---

[1] Gītā, 4.16

commentaries on the core scriptures, wrote original Vedāntic treatises like Upadeśasāhasrī and composed hymns such as Saundarya Lahirī. Moreover, he travelled the length and breadth of India by foot, held debates with proponents of other schools of thought, and started several *āśrams*. More to the point, according to his biographies, he did all of this in just a short 32 years. Similarly, Amma is always engaged in action—giving *darśan*, listening to humanity's problems on her tours of India and the West, giving advice to those who ask, etc. She practically never rests. Even if Amma has "a day off," she spends it meeting with the heads of her various humanitarian institutions and reading the personal letters that contain the troubles and prayers of her devotees. In fact, in terms of action, we cannot compare Amma to any other *mahātmā*. At best, we could compare her to Kṛṣṇa, but I am sure that Amma has engaged in more action than even he did. Therefore, from the example of these three *ātma-jñānīs* alone, we can see that "renouncing action" cannot mean at the commonly understood level of the body-mind complex.

To truly understand what is meant when the scriptures say, "renounce action," we have to remember the nature of the *ātmā*—the true "I." As discussed, the *ātmā* is neither a performer of actions, nor the reaper of their results [neither a *kartā* nor a *bhoktā*]. At best, it is the consciousness that, ever detached, enlivens the body and mind, and witnesses its performance of action and its reaping of the fruits of those actions. Thus, ultimately, "renouncing karma" means to renounce the misconception that "I"—the *ātmā*—am the "doer" or "experiencer." This means that even when the *jñānī*'s body is walking, talking and thinking, he knows that, in reality, he is not the one speaking, he is not the one moving, he is not the one thinking. His view is: "It is the body and mind that are performing these actions, and I am not the body or mind." Kṛṣṇa states this very clearly in the Gītā:

> naiva kiṁcit-karomīti yukto manyeta tattva-vit |
> paśyañcchṛṇvan-spṛśañjighrannaśnan-gacchan-svapañśvasan ||
> pralapan-visṛjan-gṛhṇannunmiṣan-nimiṣannapi |
> indriyāṇīndriyārtheṣu vartanta iti dhārayan ||

> The knower of truth should think with awareness, "I do nothing at all"–though seeing, hearing, touching, smelling, eating, going, sleeping, breathing, speaking, evacuating, holding, opening and closing the eyes–firm in the thought that this is but the senses moving among sense objects.[1]

This understanding is possible because through his knowledge the *ātma-jñānī* has disidentified with his lower self, comprised of the body, mind and senses, and identified with the higher self, the pure, blissful consciousness, which he knows to be all-pervasive and eternal. Just as the *ātma-jñānī* is able to witness the external phenomena in the world around him without any need to claim agency, so too he is able to witness his own body's actions and his own mind's thoughts without claiming agency. By the power of his understanding, he is able to transact while discriminating the body and mind from himself, the consciousness that pervades and sustains them.

Thus, while a Śrī Kṛṣṇa, a Śrī Śaṅkara or an Amma may seem to perform copious action, in reality this is only from the view of those who remain confused about the nature of the self. From Amma's perspective she is not the body that travels, gives talks, sings *bhajans* and gives *darśan*. She is the *ātmā* and has never performed an action, never reaped the fruit of an action and never will.

Aside from the testament of the lives of various *mahātmās*, there are other reasons why "renouncing karma," doesn't mean ceasing physical action. One of these, Amma has explained many times. In order to demonstrate the difference between true renunciation of action, as explained above, and false renunciation, Amma often cites the example of someone who has recently moved to an *āśram*. The person in Amma's anecdote tells the others in the *āśram* about all the things he has left behind in order to take up *āśram* life: his book collection, his nice clothing, his job, his car, his pets, etc. Ostensibly, this individual has renounced certain actions. He has stopped the action of collecting books, of wearing nice clothing, of driving a nice car, etc. To the layperson this will sound like "renouncing action."

[1] Gītā, 5.8–9

However, Amma says that all of these "non-actions" are still fully loaded with a sense of *ahaṅkāra* [identity with the body-mind complex] and its associate sense of agency. Thus, even though these "non-actions" seem to be cessation of action, in reality, they are no different from engagement in action.

In fact, there is no such thing as "nonperformance of action" at the level of the body and mind. The body and mind will always act. Even if an individual sits quiet, this is but another form of action, as it involves the individual's will, etc. Real non-performance of action can only happen through a proper understanding of our true nature. We have to understand that we are not the body or the mind but the *ātmā*, and it is only the body-mind that is performing actions and reaping their fruits, never the *ātmā*.

This is an extremely subtle truth. This is why Kṛṣṇa repeats it over and over again throughout the Gītā. In fact, it is repeated so often that, Śrī Śaṅkara feels it necessary to explain the need for the repetition. His answer is insightful. First he says it is repeated because the principle of non-agency is so subtle that it is difficult to comprehend. Then he adds another reason: Since the universe and the mechanics of human perception are constantly presenting humanity with a contrary-to-reality experience, it is very easy for the Vedāntic seeker to forget this truth. As such, he falls back into his attachment to the illusion that he is the body-mind complex and thus is the performer of actions and the enjoyer of their fruits.[1]

The question, of course, comes: What is the nature of this delusion? Why, if I am not the performer of actions, does it seem like I am? This is explained through the example of someone travelling in a vehicle like a boat. In fact, the man standing on the boat is the one who is moving. However, when he looks at the riverbank, he may have the experience that he is standing still and the scenery around him is what is moving. He thus superimposes his movement upon his inert surroundings. Vedānta says that a similar illusion is taking place with regard to humankind and its sense of agency. The only difference is

[1] Commentary on Gītā, 4.18

that instead of superimposing the action of a sentient entity (the man in the boat) upon an insentient one (the trees on the riverbank), we are superimposing the actions of our inert body and mind upon the only true sentient entity in all of existence—ourselves, the all-pervasive *ātmā*. In the same way the perception that the riverbank is moving is natural, so too is this illusion. Thus, the only way to disempower this illusion is to dwell continually in the reality of the Vedāntic teaching. Moreover, whenever the tendency arises to identify with the doer or to fret over the results that will come to us in the future, we have to recollect this teaching and remind ourselves, "This is all an illusion. I am superimposing the actions of my body and mind upon myself. In reality, I am not the performer of actions; I am the eternal witness. The fruits of actions should not make me tense because they relate only to the body and mind, and I am but pure awareness, and thus unaffected," etc.

Throughout the Gītā, Śrī Kṛṣṇa constantly advises Arjuna not to refrain from action physically. He tells Arjuna, again and again, that he should perform his work with a *karma-yoga* attitude. Moreover, if and when Arjuna becomes ready to adopt a Vedāntic outlook, he should continue to perform his duties with that enlightened Vedāntic perspective. He doesn't give Arjuna an option of stopping actions. The question thus arises, why is this an issue? Is there some scope for renouncing actions physically?

Traditionally when someone takes *sannyāsa*, he does renounce karma physically. However, this does not mean that he ceases all physical actions, but that he stops performing Vedic rites. In Kṛṣṇa's day, Indian society was still adhering to the Vedic way of life. Thus, many people were regularly performing compulsory and noncompulsory rituals. Moreover, many people were doing these rites to secure their own comfort and material prosperity, either in the here or in the hereafter. Thus, when one took *sannyāsa*, he was supposed to cease all rites—compulsory and noncompulsory. In fact, in this day and age, the topic of ceasing Vedic rites has become rather academic since hardly any one is performing Vedic rites in the first place. Therefore the most important things to understand about "renouncing karma" are: 1) maintaining awareness of the truth that the true self can never perform any action, and 2) the cessation of all actions—religious or mundane—aimed at attaining the experience of happiess and security through material ends.

Another reason the *sannyāsī* is to stop all Vedic rites is that, traditionally, he is supposed to dedicate himself to only three actions: *śravaṇam*, *mananam* and *nididhyāsanam*—studying Vedānta under his guru, clarifying his doubts and, once he has clearly understood, remaining steadfast in the Vedāntic mindset. In order to make maximum time for those activities, his other actions are to be limited to the bare minimum required for sustaining the body. It is Amma's firm stance that in the present-day world a *sannyāsī*'s life should be for service. That service can be in teaching the scriptures (which, for the teacher, is another form of *nididhyāsanam* since he is forced to dwell in the teaching just as much as, if not more than, his students) or it can be through other avenues. Amma believes a *sannyāsī* should stand firm in the awareness that he is not the body or mind and, in turn, offer those instruments completely for the upliftment of the world.

Obviously the majority of people—even the majority of spiritually inclined individuals, Amma's devotees included—are not going to take *sannyāsa*. It is a path for a very small section of society. As discussed in the chapter on *nirmamaḥ*, external *sannyāsa*—shaving one's head and donning ochre robes, etc—is not required for liberation. What is required for liberation is inner *sannyāsa*, maintaining a Vedāntic outlook and being emotionally at peace with the truth that all your forms of external security, all your relationships, all your comforts and possessions can disappear in the blink of an eye.

I remember, during Amma's 2008 North American Tour, Amma was sitting with a family of devotees. The eldest son, who had recently graduated from college, was sitting a bit back from the rest of the family. Eventually Amma called him forward and into her arms. He timidly asked Amma, "Do you have any advice for me? Any suggestions?" Amma smiled at him graciously. He then said, "Anything Amma says I will do." At this point, the father jokingly chided, "Even become a *sannyāsī*?" A serious expression came over Amma's face and she said in English, "No, no, no. Not for you. Family life is very nice. You be a *sannyāsī* in your heart. Not outside with the robes, but in your heart." This is the same advice Kṛṣṇa gives Arjuna in the Gītā, and the advice that Amma has for the majority of humanity.

Some people may ask, "Isn't renouncing karma possible through *karma yoga*?" After all, in *karma yoga*, one does not look for any *puṇyam* [karmic merit]; one performs work and *seva* only "to please God." Of course, the *karma yogī* knows that through this worship he will attain mental purity, but that is not his conscious focus. He simply works as worship, accepting whatever comes to him in life with equanimity as God's *prasādam*. Some people refer to this as "renouncing karma." However, the *karma yogī* has only renounced attachment to the material fruits of his actions, not his sense of agency or his identification with the body that experiences those actions' fruits. Such renunciation is only possible through Vedāntic understanding. However, the *karma-yoga* attitude is a crucial rung on the spiritual ladder. Without it, we can never ascend to Vedānta.

If we reflect, we can see that, with regard to action, there are three levels of mindsets presented in Sanātana Dharma: 1) I am the agent of action and the reaper of results, 2) I am doing this action as worship of the Lord alone and not out of any attempt for material benefit other than purity of mind, and I will accept whatever comes materially as the God's *prasādam*, and 3) I am not the performer of any action whatsoever, nor the reaper of any fruit; I am merely a witness of the actions of the body-mind complex. Moving to the second mindset is the beginning of spiritual life, and establishment in the third is the culmination of spiritual life. However, before one can move from mindset two to mindset three, one must not only have significantly purified his mind of likes and dislikes, he also must be completely clear on the Vedāntic teaching regarding the nature of the self. Therefore, until one has fully understood Vedānta, he really cannot enter the final mindset. He should continue to employ the *karma-yoga* attitude toward all of his actions until he has fully grasped Vedānta. For, if we have yet to clearly understand why we are not the agent, how can we possibly live maintaining such an attitude?

Thus we can never discount *karma yoga*'s essential role in the spiritual path. Moreover, we should hold on to the *karma-yoga* attitude until we have the strength and maturity to securely take hold of the Vedāntic attitude. Spiritual life is like climbing a mountain using a rope. At a certain point, we may see another rope that, ultimately, can take us higher. We can switch ropes, but first we should be confident that we have the strength to make that transition. Don't let go of the old rope until you are sure you have the second one firmly in your grasp. Without letting go of the old rope, test your grip on the new rope. That is, when difficult circumstances arise in life—ridicule, illness, defeat, censure—can we accept them remaining detached, seeing ourselves as not the one being mocked, sick, defeated, criticized? Can we get through such times without complaint, maintaining the same witness-like attitude we have towards the tragedies in the lives of strangers? If we feel we are ready to try to hold on to that attitude, then we are ready for the new Vedāntic rope. If not, we need to hold onto the *karma-yoga* rope for a bit longer. And it is not that the *karma-yoga* rope itself is so easy to hold on to! Even there, we should be able to accept those same difficulties—ridicule, illness, loss, etc—peacefully as God's will. That in itself is a great accomplishment. If we are honest, the majority of us will admit that even such an attitude is difficult for us. In fact, anytime we find ourselves praying, "Oh, Amma, please remove this problem from me; I cannot bear it," it is an indicator that we are having difficulty even hanging on to the *karma-yoga* rope. Thus, it is essential that we are honest with ourselves, understand our level and proceed from there.

Before proceeding to the next quality, we should understand the benefit of renouncing agency. While on the one hand non-agency is the truth regarding our real nature, maintaining awareness of that truth brings us an important byproduct and that is freedom from another false self-notion—the sense of being the experiencer. This pair—the false notion of the sense of agency and the false notion of the sense of being the experiencer—is inextricably linked. In order to understand this connection, we need to do some further investigation of the scriptural concepts of *karma* and *karma phalam*—action and its fruit.

Each action we perform has two effects: a perceived result and an unperceived result.[1] The perceived result is the direct physical ramifications that take place according to the laws of science and psychology. The unperceived result is what is popularly referred to as karma.[2] This result is derived not from the action but from the motivation behind the action. Unlike the perceived result, the unperceived result must ripen before it manifests. The duration is inscrutable; it could be a week, a year, a lifetime, 10 lifetimes... Regardless, all intentional human actions performed with a sense of agency eventually bear a motivation-based fruit. Selfless actions done to help others, for example, eventually produce an auspicious result. Selfish actions that harm others eventually will produce an inauspicious result. According to the scriptures, every experience that comes to us in life originates in the agent-identified motivations with which we've performed past actions. If we ask, "If all births and experiences are dictated by actions performed in the past, what about our first life?" the answer is, "There was no first life; our previous births are beginningless."

During the course of our infinite past lives, each individual has accumulated an infinite amount of karmic fruits. The scriptures divide this karma into three categories: *sañcitam*, *āgāmī* and *prārabdham.*[3] *Sañcitam* refers to the infinite pool of yet-to-fructify karmic fruit amassed from the actions an individual has performed during his infinite past lives. *Prārabdham* is the karmic fruit separated from that reservoir to fructify and be reaped in the current lifetime. *Āgāmī* is the karmic fruit created by the actions we are performing in this current life. Some *āgāmi karma* will bear fruit in this life itself, some in future births.

[1] Dṛṣṭa phalam and adṛṣṭa phalam, respectively

[2] Karma literally means "action." This is the word's primary meaning. However, in English, its secondary meaning of karma phalam—"the fruit of action"—has become its most common usage.

[3] The literal meanings of sañcitam, āgāmī and prārabdham respectively are: "that which is accumulated," "that which is impending" and "that which has commenced."

The process of karma-induced birth and death is an infinite vicious circle. This is why the scriptures refer to it as the *saṁsāra cakram*—the wheel of transmigration. As such, it may seem that, just as there is no first birth, there is also no last birth either. However, this is not the case. For, as is commonly known, self-knowledge frees one from the karmic cycle. How so?

In this context, it is common to hear people speak of "exhausting karma." Many people believe that one can only attain liberation when they have exhausted—or "burned up"—all of their past karma. While it is true that every experience—be it auspicious or inauspicious—exhausts/burns some of our karma, we have to remember that our *sañcita-karma* reservoir is infinite. Moreover, the motivations behind our current actions are only creating more *āgāmi karma*, much of which upon our death will be added to that stockpile. Thus we can see that there is no escape from the totality of the fruits of our actions via their experience.

In the Gītā, Kṛṣṇa provides us with the only solution, and that is self-knowledge:

> yathaidhāṁsi samiddho'gnirbhasmasāt-kurute'rjuna |
> jñānāgniḥ sarva-karmāṇi bhasmasāt-kurute tathā ||
>
> Just as a well-kindled fire turns all logs into ash, O Arjuna, so too the fire that is self-knowledge turns all karmas into ash.[1]

According to the scriptures, *ātma-jñānam* has several effects with regard to the fruits of karma. First, because of the *jñānī*'s disidentification with the agent, his actions immediately cease to produce *āgāmi karma*. This is because the *jñānī* identifies only with the witness consciousness, not the agent. It is the identification as the agent—the sense "I am the doer"—that produces karmic fruits. Without it, all actions are mere movement from a karmic perspective. Thus, it is the *jñānī*'s knowledge and awareness of the truth "I am not the agent" that destroys his karma's ability to bear motivation-based fruit. (Here, we should not forget that the *jñānī*'s disidentification with agency never results in

[1] Gītā, 4.37

immoral behavior, since such behavior has been eradicated by virtue of his years of self-discipline and by his self-knowledge.)

One reason Kṛṣṇa uses the example of the burnt log is that a burnt log looks more or less the same as a normal log. However, just touch it with the poker and it will crumble to ash. In the same way, the actions of the *jñānī* will look just like anyone else's actions. However, they are utterly different due the *jñānī*'s lack of sense of agency, and, as such, they do not produce karmic fruit for him either.

How is this possible? In order to understand, it is helpful for us to look at perhaps the most oft-chanted verse in the entire Bhagavad-Gītā. This verse is presented by Kṛṣṇa specifically in response to Arjuna's desire to better understand why the *ātma-jñānī*'s actions are "seedless."[1] The verse in question is from the fourth chapter:

> brahmārpaṇaṁ brahma havirbrahmāgnau brahmaṇā hutam |
> brahmaiva tena gantavyaṁ brahma-karma-samādhinā ||
>
> The oblational ladle is *brahman*. The oblation is *brahman*. The action of pouring the oblation is done by *brahman* into the fire that is *brahman*. *Brahman* alone is the attainment of one who abides in the understanding that [all aspects] of karma are *brahman*.[2]

This verse describes the understanding of the *jñānī* when he performs any action. While Kṛṣṇa uses an example of a Vedic rite, the import can be extended to any action, be it religious or mundane. An action involves six factors: 1) the agent of the action, 2) the direct object of the action, 3) the action itself, 4) the instrument with which the action is performed, 5) the physical location in which the action occurs, and 6) the result of the action. Here, Kṛṣṇa says that the *jñānī* abides in the understanding that all six of these have as their substratum the one and the same *brahman*—his own *ātmā*—and thus, ultimately, it can only be *brahman* that is temporarily appearing as all diverse

---

1 In his introductory commentary on 4.24, Śrī Śaṅkara introduces the transitional question, kasmāt punaḥ kāraṇāt kriyamāṇaṁ karma svakāryārambham akurvat samagram pravilīyate iti ucyate: "For what reason, again, does an undertaken action [by the ātma-jñānī] get totally destroyed without producing its result?"

2 Gītā, 4.24

names and forms. In this metaphor, the performer of the Vedic rite represents all agents of action. The oblation represents all direct objects of action. The action of pouring the oblation represents all actions themselves. The ladle represents all instruments involved in carrying out any action. The oblational fire represents all physical locations in which all actions take place. The karma reaped through the rite represents the results of actions—*karma phalam*. Kṛṣṇa then calls the person who performs actions with such an understanding a *brahma karma samādhi*—one who remains established in the ability to see *brahman* in all the six aspects of action.

How does this verse answer Arjuna's question regarding why the *ātma-jñānī*'s actions produce no karmic results? Śrī Śaṅkara explains from two perspectives. First, he says that since someone with such a vision sees himself as *brahman* and not as the agent of action, by the very nature of that understanding his actions become seedless. However, secondly, even if this were not the case and the *jñānī*'s actions did bring fruit, the *jñānī* would not see that fruit as having any reality. For, when one sublimates all the six aspects of action as ultimately unreal superficial projections, the karmic fruits are included in that sublimation. Thus, all experiences that come to the *jñānī* are not seen as fruits of actions, but as *brahman* cloaked in an illusory form. The spiritually ignorant may say, "The fruit is coming to the *jñānī*." At most, the *jñānī* would say, "*Brahman* is coming to *brahman*."

Here, one may get a doubt: If one does not desire any fruit, what would spur him to any action? As mentioned before, the *jñānī* does retain one desire, and that desire is his sole motivation: *loka-saṅgraha*—the upliftment of the world. Even though he knows that duality is but an illusion, nonetheless, out of compassion for those who have yet to reach his level of understanding, he continues to adhere to dharma as an example for humankind. And even if the *jñānī* becomes a reclusive *sannyāsī* and ceases to interact in society, the scriptures give him the imperative of continuing to perform the basic actions for human survival.

Thus far we have seen only why *ātma-jñānam* ceases the production of *āgāmi karma*. However, the scriptures say that it destroys the *jñānī*'s *sañcita-karma* reservoir as well. This is because upon the *jñānī*'s death, *ātma-jñānam* severs the umbilical cord, as it were, that connected him to that reservoir. As Amma often says, "If you owe someone money in a dream, when you wake up you don't still have to pay it, do you?"

This leaves us with only one more type of karma: *prārabdha karma*—the subset of karmic fruits destined to ripen and bear fruit in this lifetime itself. The scriptures say that *prārabdham* is like an already fired arrow. Thus, there is no avoiding its experience. Regardless, although he may experience physical pain or comfort according to his *prārabdham*, the *jñānī* is detached from those experiences. He sees them as happening to the body and mind, not to himself, the *ātmā*. Thus physical pain does not sway him emotionally. Actually, the idea that *prārabdham* must be endured is only from the perspective of the spiritually ignorant, never from that of the *jñānī* himself. From his perspective, self-knowledge also destroys *prārabdham* because he no longer sees it as having any reality. The *jñānī* in Kṛṣṇa's example sees all six aspects of the Vedic rite as being essentially *brahman*, and *prārabdham* is one of those aspects.

Moreover, due to the *jñānī*'s self-conception as pure consciousness, he does not view himself as the experiencer in any way, shape or form. He has rejected both poles of experience—the auspicious and the inauspicious as well as everything in between—as phenomena merely happening to the body and mind. His attitude is "I am neither of these; I am merely a witness." Thus, when the *jñānī*'s body, say, falls ill, society may say, "Oh, he is undergoing his *prārabdham*," but from the *jñānī*'s perspective, he is undergoing absolutely nothing at all. He does not connect himself with agency or with any experience. He is, was and will always be the *ātmā*, which neither acts nor experiences. At most, he is just a witness, and that too a witness to a play in which all the actors, sets, props—even the Director Himself—are but temporary names and forms projected upon the eternal substratum that is he himself.

This leads us to another important point: Although the scriptures do speak of such concepts as attaining *jīvanmukti* and *videhamukti*—liberation while living and liberation from embodiment after death—these are exclusively from the standpoint of those who have yet to attain self-knowledge. They are events set in time. *Jīvanmukti* is the event in time wherein the individual finally becomes established in identification with the *ātmā*. *Videhamukti* is the event in time wherein the body of one whose has become established in identification with the *ātmā* perishes. Thus both of these "liberations" are related to the body and mind, but not to the *ātmā*. The *jñānī* knows he is ever liberated, ever bodiless, ever mindless. Therefore, one who identifies with the *ātmā* will see neither of these "liberations" as relating to him. When time itself is an adjunct—a mere bubble, superimposed upon the self—what then to say of events taking place in time? They are but bubbles within bubbles, plays within a play, dreams within a dream.

This discussion emphasizes the wide array of potential self-conceptions and of undestandings regarding action and the fruits of action. One of the splendors of the *ātma-jñānī* is his ability to understand a person's level and to address him from that level. Along these lines Amma sometimes relates a personal anecdote. It seems at one point a man came for *darśan* and informed Amma that he was possessed by a demon. He then asked Amma if she could see the demon where it resided, looming over his shoulder. Amma very sweetly told him that there was no demon and that perhaps he was suffering from a psychological problem and should see a doctor. As soon as she said this, the man started shouting at Amma. Amma immediately changed her stance and said, "Oh, wait! Now I see him. For some reason, I couldn't see him before, but now I can." Pacifying and consoling the man thus, Amma said, even though there was indeed a demon, she would always be with him and protect him from it; he should not worry. Then the man became very happy. He said, "Before you, no one has ever understood me." Amma says, in this way, by her coming down to his level, the man was able to attain at least a relative amount of peace.

Amma typically employs this story to humorously demonstrate how we often have to come down to the level of other people in order to help them ascend—typically, a child or a spouse. However, from the supreme perspective of an *ātma-jñānī* like Amma, every single person who comes to her with any problem whatsoever is delusional. This delusion is not limited to those who come to her with personal, social and financial problems, but also those of us who come with so-called "spiritual problems"—our inability to get concentration in meditation, our frustration at our lack of peace of mind, our inability to transcend our likes and dislikes, etc.

How can that be? Because all problems are from the level of either the body or the mind. Just as the *ātma-jñānī* knows that he is not the body or mind, he knows with equal conviction that the same reality holds true for every being in creation. Just because someone believes himself to be the body-mind complex doesn't make it so. Therefore, when we approach Amma with our problems, she could say, "Actually, I don't know what you mean." As Amma sometimes explains, when someone complains to a *jñānī* about problems, it is like someone complaining to the sun about darkness. The sun doesn't even know what darkness is.

However, what would happen if Amma actually were to take this stance? What if when someone comes to her and says, "Amma, I'm going through a bad astrological period; nothing is working out," she were to respond, "Astrological period? You were never born and will never die"? What if when someone says, "My family life is a mess; everyone is always fighting," she were to respond, "Your family members are but shifting names and forms upon the pure existence that is your self. Being one with everything, how can you have a relationship with anything in this universe, much less a family?" What if when someone tells her, he isn't getting peace of mind despite his spiritual practices, she were to say, "Who cares about peace of mind? You're not the mind. Why are you concerned about that piece of inert matter? Your connection with it is an illusion"?

From Amma's supreme perspective, all of those answers are in fact the reality. However, as honest and true as they are, if Amma were to speak to us like this, we would behave just like the man who believed he was possessed when Amma told him there was no demon. We would say, "Amma, how can you say my problems are unreal?

You don't know what it's like to suffer like this!" Amma understands this. Therefore, just like she did with the insane man, she comes down to our level. She may give someone suffering from a bad astrological period a means to mitigate it. She will give us advice on how to deal with our family members and to establish more harmony in the home. Moreover, she will certainly help us adjust our spiritual practices and give us the encouragement and inspiration we need to persevere. Occasionally, if Amma feels the individual is mature enough, she may give a Vedāntic response. However, the very fact that we are presenting Amma with such problems, to some extent, demonstrates that we are not ready for a Vedāntic response.

Coming down to our level is an expression of Amma's compassion. In fact, when discussing the guru, all scriptures praise his compassion. To be a guru, one must be compassionate because if a *mahātmā* were to choose to do so, he could easily write off as an illusion this world and all of its problems, including those of everyone who approaches him. It is only because of the guru's willingness to come down to our level that we are gradually able to rise up to his. This in reality describes Amma's entire life—all of her interactions. In fact, the only time Amma rejects the problems associated with duality is when those problems come to her herself. If Amma suffers physical pain, she sees it as *māyā*—an illusion. If someone acts maliciously toward her, again, it is *māyā*. She could take everything in this world the same way, but she does not because she knows that it is only by coming down to our level that she can lift us up. However, coming down to our level, she never loses sight of the ultimate reality. In Amma's own words, "In spite of whatever is happening, I am always at peace." That is the uniqueness and glory of the *ātma-jñānī*.

One Who Views Friend & Foe, Honor & Dishonor, Heat & Cold, and the Comfortable & Uncomfortable With Equanimity

SAMAḤ ŚATRAU CA MITRE CA
TATHĀ MĀNĀPAMĀNAYOḤ
ŚĪTOṢṆA-SUKHA-DUḤKHEṢU SAMAḤ

Śrī Kṛṣṇa wants to reiterate that one of the main results of truly understanding our fundamental nature and maintaining an awareness of that understanding is that we will cease to be affected by the vicissitudes of life. The *ātma-jñānī*'s knowledge gives him the capacity to give every experience its proper import. From that enlightened perspective, a black-and-white labeling takes place: self or non-self—*ātmā* or *anātmā*. Only one thing gets the *ātmā* stamp: pure awareness-existence-bliss. All his perceptions—all the myriad people, places, things and interactions he perceives—are without exception, given the same status: *mithyā*—illusion. In this regard, his assessment is ruthless: "If I experience it, it is unreal."[1]

When a person has become rooted in such an outlook, how can he be swayed by the ups and downs of life? He has become like the philosopher-mathematician who says 1=10 because both are numbers. When you have adopted such a perspective, Kṛṣṇa says, your inner tranquility remains *samaḥ* [the same, equanimous] in all circumstances: in the presence of an enemy[2] or a friend, honor or dishonor, cold or heat, comfort or discomfort. Knowing everything to be but a passing phenomenon unable to touch your true nature, you easily accept the

[1] Unreal in the sense that it is a transient reality that cannot exist independently.

[2] As mentioned in the first verse of Amṛtāṣṭakam, the ātmā-jñānī has no enemies and treats everyone compassionately as a friend. (Gītā, 12.13: adveṣṭā sarva-bhūtānām maitraḥ karuṇa eva ca.) Regardless, others, out of jealousy, fear or misunderstanding may perceive the jñānī to be a foe.

so-called "good" and the so-called "bad" with equanimity. Just as 1=10 because both are numbers, so too good=bad because both are mere experiences.

The coldblooded codification of the universe into two groups–with "I," the eternal witness consciousness, on one side, and all experiences on the other–is the foundational division of the *jñānī*'s perception. In someone like Amma who has fully assimilated this truth, this classification does not require any effort; it is the foundation of her perception. Just as when we walk down the street we do not have to put in effort to differentiate between the world and our own physical body, so too Amma's ability to discriminate the *ātmā* from the *anātmā* is natural and spontaneous.

Here there is room for confusion because when we begin labeling things as *ātmā* and *anātmā*–self and non-self–we seem to be speaking of the universe in dualistic terms. What happened to Advaita–non-duality? Let it be clear when we say *anātmā*, we are not speaking about something separate from *ātmā*. This is why, at this stage of understanding, we typically abandon the *ātma-anātmā* terminology and begin speaking in terms of *brahman* and *mithyā*. *Brahman* is a synonym for *ātmā*. It is the eternal, blissful consciousness that is our true nature. *Mithyā* literally means "illusion," but it is not an illusion in terms of something that does not exist altogether, but rather an illusion in terms of something that is only temporary perceived. Furthermore, like all illusions, it has a real substratum. The snake seen in a rope is a momentarily perceived phenomenon superimposed upon the real substratum of the rope. You can neither say it exists nor can you completely say that it does not exist. While the snake is not real from the ultimate perspective, its essence–the rope–is real. The snake is thus unreal in that it lacks an independent existence. Its scales, its eyes, the way it coils–they all arise from the substratum of the rope. If there were no rope, there would be no snake. *Ātma-jñānam* is really the ability to see this truth–that the world, despite seeming to exist independetly from the self, is but a temporary "illusion" projected upon the substratum that is the self. Name and form are ephemeral, but their existence and our consciousness of them are very much real.

Even the happiness we experience in relation to them is ultimately a reflection of our true nature.

This is why this black-and-white rendering of the universe into *ātmā* and *anātmā* or *brahman* and *mithyā* does not render an individual coldhearted. It does not do so because although the *jñānī* knows that all names and forms are temporary illusions and are thus ultimately unreal, he also appreciates the self inherent in the their appearance. He sees how just below the changing surface of name and form lies an unchanging substratum—the pure existence that is he himself.

Initially this type of analysis can seem to be a bit of hairsplitting. After all, if the atom is the self, as it were, and molecules are comprised solely of atoms, how could it be wrong to see molecules as the self? It's not wrong to view names and forms as the self, but we should always remember that they are only temporary forms. The reason that it is important to make this distinction—the distinction between *ātma* and *anātmā*, *brahman* and *mithyā*, real and unreal, etc—is that when we regard temporary phenomena to be as real as the permanent reality of "I," then we will cease to remain tranquil in the presence of the pairs of opposites. If "the enemy and the friend," "the praise and the ridicule," "the heat and cold," "the comfort and discomfort," etc, are just as real as "I," the pure awareness, then how can I write them off as superfluous? If sickness, death, betrayal are of an equal reality to consciousness-existence-bliss how can I avoid suffering? Thus, it is an important distinction. We can see all aspects of creation as "divine" and offer them our prostrations, but we should never forget that it is their substratum, the pure existence that is one with our own self, that has divinified them. The name-and-form aspect of all creation can be said to be "real," but it is of a lower order of reality. We can even see death as God, but in order to have total peace when death comes for us, we need to remember death and dying are only of a temporary reality, and "I," the *ātmā*, am the only true and lasting reality.

Therefore, this understanding—that the world is divine, but "I," the one shared self, am of a higher reality of divinity—allows the *ātma-jñānī* to enjoy life as a *līlā*—a divine play. *Līlā* is an oft-heard and oft-used term, but to sincerely see something as a *līlā*, we must be able to remember that it is of a lower order of reality. The play—despite all its murder, betrayal, heartbreak and danger—is entertaining because I know it is ultimately unreal. If we forget that truth, then it is no longer entertainment but a nightmare. For the *ātma-jñānī*, life is exactly like a play. Friends and foes, praise and ridicule, heat and cold, comfort and discomfort are all are experienced by him, but they never disturb his mental peace because he knows they are all the same—they are all but different aspects of the movie of life. That said, seeing himself as an actor in the play, he plays his role properly.

One Who Is Free From Attachment

SAṄGA-VIVARJITAḤ

Śrī Kṛṣṇa has just said that the *ātma-jñānī* is able to remain emotionally nonreactive when confronted with the poles of human experience—being treated with friendship, being treated with enmity, being praised, being ridiculed, etc. Now, he gives a general reason for that equanimity: *saṅga-vivarjitaḥ*—the *jñānī* is free from attachment.

We have already seen the reason for the *jñānī*'s detachment, both in our discussion of the previous quality and when discussing the quality of *anapekshaḥ* [one who is free from desires]. Thus, by now, the relationship between self-ignorance, desire and emotional reaction should be clear. Joy occurs when we attain a desired experience, sorrow when we fail to. Desire for specific experiences arises when we feel emotionally unfulfilled and deem the experience to have the ability to complete us. This sense of emotional unfulfillment takes place when we mistake ourselves to be body-mind complex, which is inherently limited, finite, mortal. Understanding his true nature to be not the body-mind complex but the pure consciousness, the *jñānī* has corrected the root error that triggers this chain reaction. In the infinite imperturbable fullness that he claims as his very nature, there is no scope for him to become emotionally bound to any specific set of occurrences. Thus, he is ever detached, desireless, devoid of expectations. His sense of fulfillment is firmly rooted in the one true source of happiness—the self—and is in no way staked to events, experiences, relationships or any other happening. This is *saṅga-vivarjitaḥ*.

One Who Remains the Same in the Face of Censure & Praise

TULYA-NINDĀ-STUTIḤ

Śrī Kṛṣṇa adds another pair of opposite experiences to his list of examples: *nindā* and *stutiḥ*—censure and praise. In both circumstances, the *jñānī* is *tulyaḥ*—equanimous. Since the person Kṛṣṇa is speaking about is a *mahātmā*, it is only natural that he will often be praised, even physically worshipped. At a physical level, he may be garlanded, become the object of *pādapūjā*, be prostrated before, etc. At a verbal level, *bhajans* may be written about him, and there may be talks and books praising him. Obviously we see this in Amma's life. However, this physical and verbal adoration never contribute to the *jñānī*'s sense of completeness and fullness. Conversely, when the opposite comes, he has always remains similarly unaffected.

One Who Is Silent

MAUNĪ

The next quality of the *parābhakta* mentioned by Śrī Kṛṣṇa is *maunī*—one who is silent. Śrī Śaṅkara is quick to note this does not mean that once a person attains self-knowledge he will stop speaking. He says that it means he will have disciplined speech.[1] That is, he will speak only when it is necessary for the benefit of others.

Kṛṣṇa knew that his council was necessary to give Arjuna the resolve to fight the Mahābhārata War and, thereby, redirect society to the path of dharma. Moreover, he knew that the world would soon require a compendium of the Upaniṣadic knowledge and that his conversation with Arjuna could become the basis of that compendium. Therefore he spoke. Similarly, Śrī Śaṅkara knew that people were losing sight of the true import of the Vedas, and that confusion was obfuscating the path elucidated by them. Therefore he spoke. The same is true for Amma. She is speaking because countless people benefit from her willingness to answer their doubts regarding spirituality, from her encouraging words in times of hardship, from the guidance she provides to the project managers of the Āśram's various charitable projects. Spirituality reaches the next generation only through the words of the guru. If *ātma-jñānīs* are unwilling to speak, there will be no scope for the next generation to learn about spirituality or to clear their doubts. Therefore, although some *jñānīs* do become *maunīs* in the strictest sense of the term, it is certainly not a one-to-one correspondence.

What is one-to-one with *ātma-jñānam* is the cessation of self-serving speech. If we introspect, we will see that the majority of our speech is part of our general attempt to gain contentment. Discontentment is rooted in insecurity and desire. Therefore, consciously or subconsciously, people are constantly trying various means to remove that sense of insecurity and to fulfill their desires.

[1] saṁyata-vāk

Sometimes we accomplish these ends through physical action, but we also—especially in this day and age—do it through speaking and other forms of communication, including social media. We even speak to simply relieve the mental pressure created by not speaking. Since the *jñānī* has found security and joy in their one true source—the self—he is ever content, and his speech ceases to continue as a method of generating contentment.

We should understand that for one like Amma whose entire worldview is established in self-knowledge, judicious speech or even total silence is not a product of a mental resolve but is merely the natural effect of that wisdom. Regardless, for those of us who still need to purify our minds, taking a vow of silence one day a week, etc, can be helpful in our efforts to develop mental discipline. Unnecessary speaking dissipates a lot of energy that can be conserved and then used toward spiritual ends. Furthermore, only when we reduce the quantity of our speech can we hope to increase its quality, which is the more important spiritual practice. This is something Kṛṣṇa speaks about in detail in the 17th chapter:

> anudvegakaraṁ vākyaṁ satyaṁ priya-hitaṁ ca yat |
> svādhyāyābhyasanaṁ caiva vāṅmayam tapa ucyate ||
>
> The speech that causes no pain, that is truthful, pleasant and beneficial, as well as the practice of self-study—these are said to form verbal austerity.[1]

Kṛṣṇa is saying that if we are trying to practice control over our speech, we should ensure that it fulfills the four following criteria: *anudvegakaram*—it should not be hurtful to others; *satyam*—it should be truthful; *priyam*—it should be sweet to the ear of those listening; and *hitam*—it should be beneficial. As stated, such refined speech will be natural for the *jñānī*. However, until we assimilate self-knowledge and speech discipline becomes natural for us, we should strive to maintain such standards in all of our various forms of communication.

---

[1] Gītā, 17.15

One Who Is Content With Anything

SAṀTUṢṬAḤ YENA KENACIT

The next quality is *saṁtuṣṭaḥ yena kenacit*—being content with anything. The *ātma-jñānī*'s contentment is rooted in his ability to appreciate his own self as the source of all happiness. Thus he remains at peace with whatever comes or doesn't come to him in life.

When discussing this quality, Śrī Śaṅkara stresses in particular the lifestyle of the *sannyāsī*. He says, even in that austere lifestyle, wherein one's survival depends completely upon the goodwill of others in terms of food, clothing and shelter, the *jñānī*'s attitude is always "enough"—both in terms of receiving and not receiving his basic needs. Thus, when someone gives a tasty meal, his attitude is to be content with what is given and not want more; and also when someone gives a bland meal or even when his attempts at begging a meal end in failure, his attitude is also "enough." He never complains.[1]

Although Amma never formally took *sannyāsa*, we see in her its epitome. She abides in constant awareness of her true nature, she accepts everything that comes to her, and all of her actions, words and resolves are not for personal gain but for the upliftment of the world. Amma has never asked anyone for anything—food, clothing, shelter. In terms of these basic necessities, she has simply accepted what she has been given and always with this "enough" attitude.

Before we disciples began living with Amma and ensuring she was offered wholesome meals (which, regardless, Amma often barely touches), she at times subsisted only on grass. She would wear sāris that her sisters had discarded because they had tears in them, stitching

[1] According to sannyāsa dharma scriptures, there are different types of resolves a sannyāsī can make with regard to mendicancy. Some, like Amma did, will only take food when it is offered without asking. This is called ajagara vṛtti because one eats like a python [ajagara]—only when food comes to it. Another type of begging is called madhukāra vṛtti, wherein one seeks food, going from house to house like a bee [madhukāra] going from flower to flower. Even here, unlike the bee, a sannyāsī must make a resolve ahead of time as to how many houses he will visit for this purpose. If the maximum number of houses is reached and no food is offered, he must fast.

them up herself. If her family was disturbed by her singing devotional songs in the house, she would happily go outside and spend the night singing under the stars. Even the rain did not bother her. Sometimes, when Amma was outside she would sit in deep meditation, oblivious to the world around her. At such times, a few devoted neighbors would sometimes place food by her for her to eat when she came out of these exalted states of mind. Often, by the time Amma would open her eyes, the crows would have torn open the food packets and scattered and eaten the food. Even then, Amma would accept. She would never send word to the devotees to bring more food. Her attitude is, was and always will be "enough." That is true contentment with regard to anything that is received. Such an attitude comes naturally to the *jñānī*.

One Who Is Homeless

ANIKETAḤ

Śrī Kṛṣṇa continues to speak about the supreme devotee in terms of *sannyāsa*, adding that he is *aniketaḥ*—one without a home. As discussed previously, external renunciation of family and home is not a required discipline for liberation. Many people have attained self-knowledge without taking to monasticism. What is an inescapable spiritual practice and what will be a constant correlate with self-knowledge, however, is the attitude of seeing both everywhere and nowhere as one's home. As Amma says, "Not everyone needs to become a *sannyāsī*, renouncing everything. What needs to be renounced is the sense of 'I' and 'mine.'"

Several years ago when Amma was having her annual programs in Manhattan, a reporter came to interview her at the devotee's house where she and several other members of the tour group were staying. That particular devotee lived in an uptown penthouse, and the reporter commented on how posh the accommodation was. I was a bit irritated because it seemed like he was taking a soft shot at the fact that Amma was staying in such a posh home. The fact of the matter is that Amma's room in Amritapuri is an extremely humble one-bedroom flat, and on her foreign tours Amma primarily stays in small windowless rooms in the program halls themselves. Even when she does stay in a hotel, she stays in one small room. Moreover, I've been present on many occasions when Amma has given up her own accommodation for others and slept outside instead. When the reporter asked this, Amma smiled and graciously told him that she never looks at the grandeur or lack thereof of a devotee's house and that, from her perspective, no matter where she is staying—be it Amritapuri or in a hotel room or at a devotee's house—she sees it like staying in a hotel. Amma said, "When you stay in a hotel, you are happy when you come, happy when you are staying there and happy when you leave. This is because you come there with the intention of eventually leaving. You know it's only temporary and not your real home."

Rooted in her Vedāntic understanding, Amma's sense of non-ownership is so thorough that she can literally vacate and walk away from anywhere without giving it a moment's thought. In fact, for many trying to exercise external renunciation, such detachment remains elusive. I remember once an *āśram* resident decided he wanted to move to one of Amma's remote satellite *āśrams* in order to live in a hut and exclusively practice meditation. He took Amma's blessings and relocated. About a month later, the Amritapuri accommodation office sent him an email telling him that the items he had left behind in his allocated room in Amritapuri Āśram would be packed up and stored elsewhere so that someone else could live there. The person who sent the email figured that he wouldn't even hear back from the "hut-dweller" for months since he was now living such an austere "off-the-grid" lifestyle. To his surprise, he received a call from the hut-dweller's mobile phone just 30 minutes later. "You can't pack up my things! That's my room!" This reveals how easy it is to become attached to our possessions, even ones that we aren't even actively using.

The *ātma-jñānī*'s non-possessiveness comes from his understanding of his true nature. Identifying with witness consciousness, he cannot claim ownership even of his own body and mind, much less a room or a house. As Amma beautifully says, "Children, I have no particular place to dwell. I dwell in your hearts." While from the empirical standpoint of reality, this statement has one particular truth to it, from the Vedāntic angle Amma is saying, "Children, I know my true nature to be the self—the non-localized, unfragmented consciousness serving as the foundation of all plurality. Being the very substratum of time and space, how could I ever be limited to one location? I pervade everywhere as existence, consciousness, bliss and can be tangibly experienced as the eternal witness reflected in the mind of each and every individual."

Anyone can make such statements. However, if one really has such self-understanding, it will be impossible to maintain a sense of possessiveness with regard to anything. We will not only "talk the talk," we will "walk the walk." Thus, internal *sannyāsa* is a natural fruit of self-knowledge.

Although accepting that a householder can attain liberation, Śrī Śaṅkara often stresses the importance of not only internal but also external *sannyāsa*. This can be a bit disconcerting for non-*sannyāsīs*. Therefore, I think it is worth delving into the reasons for Śrī Śaṅkara's stress on monasticism. First, we have to remember that in Śrī Śaṅkara's day, householder life was synonymous with *karma yoga* and *sannyāsa* was synonymous with Vedānta. Couple this with the fact that one of the main emphases of Śrī Śaṅkara's commentaries is that liberation only comes from Vedāntic knowledge,[1] and it is easy to see why they stress *sannyāsa*. For Śaṅkara, the term *sannyāsa* was tantamount to stressing Vedāntic study and assimilation.

Secondly, in Śrī Śaṅkara's time there was a school of thought that was adamant that liberation did not come only from knowledge but from a simultaneous combination of knowledge and Vedic karmas.[2] It was Śrī Śaṅkara's mission to eradicate this misconception. Since Vedic karmas can only be performed by a householder—never by *sannyāsī*—it was helpful for Śrī Śaṅkara's "thesis" to stress the attainment of liberation by *sannyāsī*. This is because while a traditional householder can study Vedānta, he must also perform Vedic karmas. When such a person attains liberation, an external observer cannot say without a doubt that it was his Vedāntic knowledge that caused it. It could have been his Vedāntic knowledge. It also could have been his Vedic karmas. And it also could have been a combination of the two. Thus the householder makes for an inconclusive study example because of lack of adequate controls. However, when a *sannyāsī* who has renounced Vedic karmas attains liberation, there is no doubt as to the cause since all the other potential factors have been removed. In the *sannyāsī*, self-knowledge has been isolated as the only possible cause. Whereas the householder was taking two or three medicines when his disease was cured, the *sannyāsī* was only taking one.

---

[1] Śrī Śaṅkara never discounts spiritual practices such as meditation on form and *karma yoga*. He says such spiritual practices are meant to prepare the mind for Vedāntic study and assimilation. However, ultimately it is the understanding "I am brahman and the world is mithyā" alone that actually liberates.

[2] Jñāna-karma samuccaya vāda

Regardless, as Amma always stresses, the most important thing is not external renunciation, but inner renunciation. That is, attaining self-knowledge and cultivating the inner sense of non-possessiveness that is the byproduct of that knowledge—a sense of non-possessiveness not only with regard to external possessions and relationships but even with regard to our body and mind.

One Who Is Firm in Knowledge

STHIRAMATIḤ

If we look at the Vedāntic knowledge, or lack thereof, of a human being, we can say that at any given time one will reside in one of four stages of spiritual evolution. In the first stage, one identifies with the body and mind and never seriously considers that his self-concept is flawed and that he could be something other than the amalgam of these two components. Stage two is when one believes in the concept of "being the *ātmā*" or of "having a soul," but remains confused as to what that actually means. Stage three is when one has a clear understanding of what is meant by *ātmā*, why the *ātmā* is his true nature, and all the implications of that truth with regard to the world he perceives around him. Technically, at this stage, we can call the person an *ātma-jñānī*. However, despite having learned Vedānta and the correct way of viewing himself, God and the world, this person may still have to struggle to maintain that perspective. He understands that perspective and desires to maintain it, but due to habit he keeps slipping back into his ignorant way of evaluating himself and the world. Consequently he keeps reacting as per that ignorance. Only when the maintenance of the Vedāntic perspective has become one's natural, effortless, spontaneous way of viewing himself and the world does one enter the final stage and become like Amma. This final stage is given various names in various places in the scriptures. Regardless, this is what Kṛṣṇa is indicating by *sthiramatiḥ*—one firm in knowledge.

Thus, this final quality stated by Śrī Kṛṣṇa is not so much a quality per se, but rather a proclamation that to truly be considered a *parābhakta*, it is not enough merely to have learned the content of the scriptures; one must have assimilated that knowledge to the full extent. That is, the Vedāntic mindset must have become the natural, continuous state of abidance. This alone is supreme devotion.

Moreover, only when one has attained to this level, will all the the qualities that have been mentioned by Kṛṣṇa in the Amṛtāṣṭakam blossom to their full flower as one's natural characteristics. This is something stated in an important treatise by one of Śrī Śaṅkara's direct disciples:

> utpannātma-prabodhasya tvadveṣṭṛṛtvādayo guṇāḥ
> ayatnato bhavantyasya na tu sādhana-rūpiṇaḥ
>
> Indeed, to the one in whom awareness of the self has arisen, the qualities of "absence of hatefulness," etc, surely come without effort, not in the form of spiritual practices.[1]

If we review all the qualities mentioned by Kṛṣṇa throughout the Amṛtāṣṭakam, we will see that they are almost all ramifications of the assimilation of two core truths: "I am not the body-mind complex but the pure existence-consciousness-bliss" and "Everything I perceive in the world around me is an expression of my own true self but with various temporary names and forms." Assimilation of the first truth results in peaceful detachment with regard to any possible problem relating to the body-mind complex. The second results in compassionate assistance to all beings. The more "firm in knowledge" we become with regard to these truths, the more spontaneously and naturally the qualities of the Amṛtāṣṭakam will shine forth from within us. As Amma says, "When there is true love, everything is effortless."

[1] Naiṣkarmyasiddhiḥ of Sureśvarācārya, 4.69

Concluding Verse

ye tu dharmyāmṛtam-idaṁ yathoktaṁ paryupāsate |
śraddadhānā mat-paramā bhaktāste'tīva me priyāḥ ||

However, those who follow this aforementioned immortal dharma, endowed with faith, considering me as the supreme goal—those devotees are extremely dear to me.

With the previous quality, Śrī Kṛṣṇa concluded this list of characteristics by saying the supreme devotee will be a *sthiramatiḥ*—a person of firm knowledge. Thus, the list culminates with no room for doubt: Only an *ātma-jñānī* whose worldview has been permanently and firmly readjusted by his self-knowledge can truly be considered a *parābhakta*.

The reason why the *ātma-jñānī* alone can be called a supreme devotee was explained in the Introduction. First, having attained permanent emotional fulfillment through his knowledge, he seeks nothing from God, not even liberation. Secondly, since only a person with self-knowledge views God and himself as one, only such a person will be capable of loving God in the spontaneous and unwavering manner that is the exclusive domain of "self love." These are the same reasons why Kṛṣṇa says that God loves the *jñānī* more than anyone else:

caturvidhā bhajante māṁ janāḥ sukṛtino'rjuna |
ārto jijñāsurarthārthi jñānī ca bharatarṣabha ||
teṣāṁ jñānī nitya-yukta eka-bhaktirviśiṣyate |
priyo hi jñānino'tyartham-aham sa ca mama priyaḥ ||
udārāḥ sarva evaite jñānī tvātmaiva me matam |
āsthitaḥ sa hi yuktātmā mām-evānuttamāṁ gatim ||

Four types of virtuous people worship me, O Arjuna: the one in distress, the one seeking knowledge, the one seeking wealth and the *jñānī*, O best of Bharatas. Of these, the *jñānī*, ever-firm and of one devotion, excels. For I am exceedingly dear to the *jñānī*, and he is dear to me. Noble indeed are all of these, but the *jñānī*

> I deem to be my very self. For, steadfast in mind, he is established in me alone, as the supreme goal.[1]

However, the *ātma-jñānī* who is "firm in wisdom" no longer requires spiritual instruction. Nor does he need to study the Gītā. Nor does he need to hear that he is dear to God. For, he is steeped in oneness with God. His love for God is his love for his own self, and his love of his own self is God's love for him. Thus, he requires no such confirmation. On the contrary, the one who needs to be reminded that he is "dear to God" is the seeker. Thus, it is with the emotional needs of the seeker in mind that Kṛṣṇa concludes the Amṛtāṣṭakam with this final verse, wherein, in essence, he says, "Don't worry if you're not firm in wisdom. Don't worry if you aren't even a *jñānī* in any capacity of the term whatsoever. Even if you are just striving to attain these characteristics, you are still very dear to me."

Amma says the same thing. She understands our limitations, accepts us and has the patience to lift us up. Thus, of course, we are dear to her. Failing to see Amma as one with our own self, we may not have supreme devotion to Amma, but Amma definitely has supreme devotion to us.

Literally, what Kṛṣṇa says is: *tu*—However; *ye paryupāsate*—whoever follows; *idaṁ yathoktaṁ dharmya amṛtam*—this aforementioned immortal dharma; *śraddadhānāḥ*—endowed with faith; *mat-paramāḥ*—with me as their supreme goal; *te bhaktāḥ*—those devotees; *me atīva priyāḥ*—are extremely dear to me.

By saying, "however," Kṛṣṇa is indicating that, now, he no longer speaking about the person of firm knowledge. He is no longer speaking about someone for whom all these spiritual qualities—non-hatred of all beings, a universal display of friendship, compassion, etc—are not spiritual practices but spontaneous expressions. That topic is over. With this concluding verse of the Amṛtāṣṭakam, Kṛṣṇa is speaking about someone who is still struggling to live up to those qualities. Thus, he says, "Whoever just strives to follow these qualities, he is also extremely dear to me."

---

[1] Gītā, 7.16–18

Kṛṣṇa gives these qualities a specific name, and it is from this name that these eight verses have come to be called the Amṛtāṣṭakam. That name is *dharmyāmṛtam*. *Dharmya* means that which is in concordance with dharma; *amṛtam* means immortal. These qualities are thus termed because they are in line with dharma[1] and, furthermore, when the seeker strives to live by them, they will lead him to *ātma-jñānam*, upon attaining which he "gains immortality"–i.e. he comes to understand that he is the *ātmā*, that he was never born and can never die.

In fact more than anything else, Amma stresses the importance of cultivating non-hatred, compassion, forgiveness and other such universal values. She says that they are a priceless treasure that we must ever put in effort to attain. Along these lines, I recently read a newspaper article about a man who was eating at a restaurant when he saw two street children peering at him through the window. Instead of ignoring them, he called them inside and ordered them lunch, taking satisfaction in their smiles and full stomachs. When he received the check, he found not a bill but a note from the manager. It read, "Our cash register has no charge for compassion." While self-knowledge is the ultimate goal of spiritual life, its foundation is compassion. As Amma says, "Compassion is both the beginning and the culmination of spiritual life." This is the meaning of *dharmyāmṛtam*–the immortal values that both lead to immortality and are an expression of it as well.

However, it is not enough to just follow these qualities. Within this final verse, Kṛṣṇa embeds two more criteria. He says such people should be *śraddadhānāḥ*–endowed with *śraddhā*–and should *mat-paramāḥ*–see God as their ultimate goal in life.

[1] The fact that these qualities–be they undertaken as spiritual practices or be they spontaneous expressions of self-knowledge–are in line with dharma is stated because when taken from an orthodox view they can point to the taking of sannyāsa and the subsequent cessation of performance of Vedic rites. Since there are places in the Vedas wherein it is said Vedic rites should be performed yāvajjīvam–"till death," Kṛṣṇa wants to make it clear that, if one takes sannyāsa, his dharma is modified to encompass such renunciation. Thus, for him, cessation of rites is dharmyam–in line with dharma.

Śraddhā means faith in the scriptures and words of the guru.[1] The foundation of spiritual life is faith. Without it, we can never move forward. This is not to say Vedānta is illogical. It is logical, but its logic is applied to information that can only be learned from the guru and scriptures. Just as pure logic is applied to the data collected by our senses from the external world, we apply the same logical rules to the data collected from the guru and scriptures. Thus, faith is essential.

Mat-parāḥ means "those who see me as the supreme goal." No matter where we are in the spiritual path, until we firmly abide in the awareness that liberation is our true nature, we must always keep that as our primary goal. Even while practicing *karma yoga* with the immediate goal of "pleasing God," in our back pocket should be the understanding that this is all in service to our ultimate goal of abiding in our identity with God. As Amma says, "No matter who we are or what we are doing, the duties we perform in the world should help us reach the supreme dharma, which is oneness with the universal self. All living beings are one because life is one, and life has only one purpose. Owing to identification with the body and mind, one may think, 'To seek the self and attain self-realization is not my dharma; my dharma is to work as a musician or an actor or a businessman.' It is okay if one feels this way. However, we will never find fulfillment unless we direct our energy toward the supreme goal of life."

As long as our ultimate focus is not liberation, peace will elude us because it is only when we align our lives with the ultimate dharma that we can live in tune with a truly universal harmony. When things are going our way, we may be satisfied with lesser goals, but when adversity strikes, that satisfaction will start crumbling.

Remaining intent on the goal is crucial in spiritual life. The more focus we have, the faster our progress. It is our focus on the goal that serves as the fuel for all of our other spiritual practices. Amma is providing us with all the guidance and support we could possibly need. Amma's life and teachings, as well ancient scriptures like the Bhagavad-Gītā, are ever ready to remind us that everything

[1] Tattva Bodhaḥ, 1.3.5: guru vedānta-vākyādiṣu viśvāsaḥ śraddhā—"Faith in the words of the guru and Vedāntic scriptures is śraddhā."

we are seeking is in fact our true self. To gain inspiration, we need to remain focused and regularly spend time with those sources of supreme knowledge. May Amma's grace bless our efforts to attain this infinite wisdom.

|| om lokāḥ samastāḥ sukhino bhavantu ||

May all the beings in all the worlds be happy.

Pronunciation Guide

The letters with dots under them (ṭ, ṭh, ḍ, ḍh, ṇ, ḷ) are palatal consonants; they are pronounced with the tip of the tongue against the hard palate. Letters without such dots are dental consonants and are pronounced with the tongue against the base of the teeth. In general consonants are pronounced with very little aspiration unless immediately followed by an h (kh, gh, th, dh, ph, bh, etc.), in which case aspiration is strong.

a like the a in America
ā like the a in father (vowel is extended)
i like the ea in heat
ī like the ee in beet (long vowel)
u like the ui in suit
ū like the oo in pool (long vowel)
e like the a in gate (always long in Sanskrit)
o like the o in opinion (always long in Sanskrit)
ai like the ai in aisle
au like the ow in how
ṛ like the ri in river (usually not rolled)
kh like the kh in bunkhouse (hard aspiration)
gh like the gh in loghouse (hard aspiration)
ṅ like the n in sing
c like the c in cello
ch like the ch in charm (hard aspiration)
jh like the j in just (hard aspiration)
ñ like the ny in canyon
th like the t in table (hard aspiration, tongue at base of teeth)
dh like the dh in redhead (hard aspiration, tongue at base of teeth)
ph like the ph in shepherd or like the f in fun
bh like the bh in clubhouse
v like the v in victory (but closer to a w)
śa like the ci in efficient
ṣa like the sh in shut
ḥ echoes preceding vowel

CPSIA information can be obtained
at www.ICGtesting.com
Printed in the USA
LVOW04s1052081016
507958LV00015B/604/P